Believing GOD

Studies on Faith in Hebrews 11

R.T. KENDALL

MorningStar
PUBLICATIONS
P.O. Box 19409
Charlotte, NC 28219-9409

Believing God

by R.T. Kendall

Copyright © 1997 by R.T. Kendall

First reprint: October 1999

Printed in the United States of America.

International Standard Book Number 1-878327-63-1.

MorningStar Publications & Ministries
P.O. Box 19409
Charlotte, NC 28219-9409

MorningStar's Website: www.morningstarministries.org

For information call 704-522-8111.

Table of Contents

PREFACE

One evening in October 1977, I was driving with Dr. Martyn Lloyd-Jones to Chipping Norton. I asked him to come up with a definition of faith that would introduce and carry me through my new series of sermons on Hebrews 11. We tossed around several apt definitions, both before and after the sermon he preached later that night.

The next day the telephone rang, and I answered it. "Believing God," the familiar voice replied on the other end. "Believing God. That's your definition." I knew at once that I would do no better than that. So I adopted Dr. Lloyd-Jones's definition—then and now.

What follows is not a book of sermons in the strictest sense. Although the thirty chapters are derived from thirty-seven sermons based upon the eleventh chapter of the Epistle to the Hebrews (which I preached in Westminster Chapel on Sunday mornings beginning in October 1977), I have virtually rewritten them all.

Those who have read *Jonah* (Hodder and Stoughton, 1978) will recall that it is a book of sermons with almost no editing. The reader can decide which style is better, but after reading the transcript of my second series in Westminster (as typed from a tape recorder), I decided that my preaching on Hebrews 11 would bear more attention.

Apart from a slightly different style, the main change to be found here (compared to the original sermons) is my giving less detail to verses 13 to 16 and verses 33 to 40. This is how the thirty-seven sermons were condensed to thirty chapters. This book focuses on the mighty stalwarts of faith, those **"who by faith"** (Greek *hoi dia pisteos*, verse 33) did wonderful things.

I have sought, nonetheless, to remind the reader frequently that the writer of the Epistle to the Hebrews was more concerned about the nature of faith than about these people of faith. It was his thesis regarding faith itself that lay behind his bringing in these men and women in the first place. To overlook this would be to miss not only our writer's own purpose but also some important theological principles.

This book has been affectionately dedicated to Dr. and Mrs. Janos Harlan Milby of Brentwood, Tennessee. The Milbys have been like a second set of parents and have stood by my family and me faithfully for many years. Our sojourn at Oxford was made humanly possible by their prayers and financial support. I trust they will enjoy reading this book, which has as much to say about heaven as about faith: their only son Tom reached that "**city which has foundations**" twenty-five years ago.

My deepest debt however, as always, is to my wife and children. It was difficult to avoid being personal in Chapter 9, for I do identify with Abraham to a considerable degree. Yet, we all admit that with every passing day, living in England is becoming less and less like "**sojourning in a strange country.**"

R.T. Kendall
London
September 1980

Chapter One

WHAT IS FAITH?

Hebrews 11:1

Now faith is the substance of things hoped for, the evidence of things not seen.

"We have not lost faith," George Bernard Shaw once said, "but we have transferred it from God to the medical profession!"

What is faith? Surely there is no more crucial subject to be considered at the present time, and yet there is hardly one on which so much confusion abounds. Modern man and the modern church, generally speaking, are so far removed from the biblical view of faith that even George Bernard Shaw's statement is more theological than many sermons heard today. It is a day in which the church's faith has become man-centered and, consequently, the average church member has very little grasp of genuine faith.

The church at the present time may be justly described as having lost its faith. This loss of faith is the best explanation for the state of the world. For Jesus said to the church, **"Ye are the *salt* of the earth."** The chaos and turmoil of the world are traceable to the state of the church. But if the salt loses its savor, it is **". . . good for nothing, but to be cast out, and to be trodden under foot of men"** (Matt. 5:13).

The eleventh chapter of the Epistle to the Hebrews, well known as the "faith" chapter of the Bible, in fact describes the only kind of valid faith there is. Any faith other than that which is depicted in Hebrews 11 is a spurious faith, whether the object of such faith be the medical profession or a false God. This is not to say that the events described are the only ones in which faith may be present, but there is to be seen in that great chapter a cohesive principle to which each of those stalwarts was consciously connected. If we today are not joined to the same principle, it follows that our own faith is counterfeit.

In this chapter, I want not only to show what that principle is but also to encourage the reader to know of the happy possibility of having the same faith that motivated and upheld these remarkable men. Hebrews 11 would have no meaning or relevance at all if it were not possible to do the same things which they did. But because Jesus Christ is the **"same yesterday, to day, and for ever" (Heb. 13:8)** and He promised, **"I will never leave thee, nor forsake thee" (Heb. 13:5),** it is the thesis of this book that we may serve the same God as these heroes served and that we can do the same things that they did. Hebrews 11 is not a museum but a living experience and fellowship. I believe it is possible to know the true God so intimately that the heroes in this chapter become alive to us as though living relatives. The Apostle John implies such a kinship: **"I John, who also am your brother, and companion in tribulation" (Rev. 1:9).**

Getting to Know the God of the Heroes

The first principle to be grasped, then, is that if we are to have their faith, we must know their God. We cannot have the effect without the cause, or their results without their dedication. Neither can we be selective with the various heroes of faith and try to imitate one or two of them pragmatically to get through a particular situation. These men were connected to a principle that gave each of them something in common: Each of them was tuned in to the same frequency.

What any one of them did the others could have done had they been in a similar situation. For they were initially faithful **"in that which is least"** that they might also be **"faithful in much" (Luke 16:10).** Thus, not one of these was by nature any more spectacular than the next. If we, too, are faithful in that which is least, we will do in our day what they did in theirs.

We therefore must be sure that we are acquainted with their God. If we are not, then all that they did will make them seem supernatural (which they were not). If we do not know their God as they did, then we can but admire them from afar, and Hebrews 11 becomes little more than a wax museum. These men were real men, but so was their God real. This God is the living God and wants to know men today as intimately as He knew these men. Such, indeed, is a happy possibility.

The writer of our chapter began it with a general definition of faith: **"Now faith is the substance of things hoped for, the evidence of things not seen."** Whether this verse ought to have been the concluding verse of Hebrews 10 or put precisely where it is, has been questioned. But, in any case, one should not try to understand Hebrews 11:1 apart from the context of the epistle as a whole. What is also open to question is whether the writer intended to give a final definition of faith in Hebrews 11:1. It is our task to understand this verse in its context; we shall also adopt a more succinct definition of faith later on in this chapter.

The Epistle to the Hebrews might be best understood as one continuous exhortation (see Heb. 13:22) to Christians who had witnessed many of their friends go back into the world after making a profession of faith in Jesus Christ. These Christians who remained were discouraged and were tempted to wonder if they too had made a mistake by staying with the church. The writer addresses the remnant and does so with a two-fold exhortation: a warning and an encouragement. He warns them that if they too **"draw back" (Heb. 10:30),** they need not expect to be in any better state than those who had fallen away (Heb. 6:4-6).

Thus in Hebrews we find some of the most dreadful warnings to be found anywhere in Holy Writ (see Heb. 2:1-3; 3:10-12; 4:1; 10:26-31). And yet no more tender words of encouragement can be found anywhere (see 2:9; 4:16; 6:9-10; 10:35-37). In this context of great encouragement comes the eleventh chapter of Hebrews.

We need to look at this immediate context more carefully. For if we grasp this we will have a greater measure of understanding of our central theme. Having said, **"Cast not away therefore your confidence, which hath great recompence of reward" (Heb. 10:35),** the writer sets before them the possibility that God Himself will visit them in a most wonderful and familiar way. **"For yet a little while, and he that shall come will come, and will not tarry" (Heb. 10:37).**

This was a promise that the Lord, who at the moment was hiding His face, would shortly manifest Himself to them in such measure and reality that no room would be left for doubting or discouragement. The writer urges them, "Hold on. Keep on. Go on. Do not lose heart." He thus alludes to Habakkuk 2:3: **"For the vision is yet for an appointed time, but at the end it shall speak, and not lie: though it tarry, wait for it; because it will surely come, it will not tarry."** God had promised Habakkuk there would be a moment in time when no further waiting would be necessary— there would come a time when the glory of God would be openly revealed and manifested.

Waiting in Faith

But what does one do in the meantime? One waits. One waits patiently. Why? Because one believes God. One believes that God is faithful. One believes that God will not lie. One waits for God—or lives by the faithfulness of God—to keep His promise. So Habakkuk concluded that **"the righteous shall live by his [God's] faithfulness" (Hab. 2:4 NIV margin).**

The translation from the Hebrew makes this clear. The Septuagint (the Greek translation of the Old Testament) translated this simply, **"The just shall live by faith,"** and the New Testament citations appear to refer back to the Septuagint rather than the original Hebrew. In any case, the context of Habakkuk 2:1-4 and Hebrews 10:35-38 shows clearly that the ground for waiting patiently was God's faithfulness. Such waiting or enduring, then, is called *faith*. It was faith in God's faithfulness.

It is at this stage that the writer makes this general statement about faith, that it is **"the substance of things hoped for, the evidence of things not seen" (Heb. 11:1).** While it may be called a definition, speaking generally, it is really more of a description of faith. It is like saying that the sky is blue, or water is wet, or fire is hot. And yet it is a necessary statement, for it sums up what he means by waiting on God while God hides Himself. He describes such waiting as being a most positive thing, for the one who waits on God believes in his heart of hearts that God is faithful.

This is why the writer says that faith is the **"substance"** *(hypostasis)* of things hoped for. This Greek word may be translated **"assurance."** The New International Version says: **"Now faith is being sure of what we hope for."** The point is this: Faith is that which keeps us looking beyond what we can see with our natural senses, with such confidence that we know we shall not be disappointed. Faith looks beyond oneself, never within oneself. Faith always leads us outside ourselves. Why? Because faith perceives its object—God.

The main insight the writer's statement conveys, however, is what faith is *not*. It is the **"evidence of things not seen."** The Greek is *pragmaton elegchos ou blepomenon*—literally, **"persuasion of the works not seen."** One is convinced that one will see them; one is truly persuaded that one will see them. But one does not see them at the moment. Therefore, faith is *not seeing* the tangible. If one sees now what one previously had been waiting for, it ceases to be called faith.

Until what someone was waiting for literally appears, such waiting is graced with the title *faith*. But if the vision ceases to tarry (see Hab. 2:3) and is now fulfilled, it can no longer be called faith. Seeing, then, is not believing; seeing is the opposite of faith. The expression "seeing is believing" is not true of genuine faith. For if one sees, it can no longer be called faith.

Yet, faith is nonetheless to be **"certain of what we do not see"** (NIV). There is an element of certainty and assurance in faith. Why can one be so certain? Because one is persuaded of the integrity of God to keep His promise. **"For yet a little while, and he that shall come will come, and will not tarry" (Heb. 10:37).** The one who believes God knows he will not be deceived. He waits. He **"staggers not at the promise of God"** but is **"fully persuaded that, what he had promised, he was able also to perform" (Rom. 4:20-21).**

Believing God

This is the meaning of the writer to the Hebrews. From what we have seen so far, then, we may conclude that faith is *believing God*. This is our definition of faith throughout this book: believing God. **"For what saith the scripture? Abraham *believed God*, and it was counted unto him for righteousness" (Rom. 4:3).** Paul also said, **"Wherefore, sirs, be of good cheer: for I *believe God*, that it shall be even as it was told me" (Acts 27:25).** "Ye are my witnesses, saith the Lord, and my servant whom I have chosen: that ye may know and *believe* me, and understand that I am He" (Isa. 43:10).**

The heroes of Hebrews 11 are people who believed God. They are the writer's examples to show that faith itself is not a New Testament innovation. Faith goes way back in time, claims the writer of Hebrews. There is nothing new about it at all. God hides His face in order that we might believe. He withholds the evidence of things visible, that we might be persuaded by His Word alone!

Faith, then, is the long parenthesis between the undeniable appearances of God's glory. When God appears, faith is no longer necessary. There are actually times when faith is eclipsed by such a sense of the majesty and glory of God that one is temporarily without the need of faith. These times are mountaintop experiences, such as when our Lord was transfigured before His disciples (Matt. 17:1-9).

But one is not permitted to live indefinitely on the mountaintops. Like the disciples who **"came down from the mountain" (Matt. 17:9)**, so must we. It is in the valley that we live by the faithfulness of God, who periodically reveals Himself so we will not be swallowed up in despair.

These Hebrew Christians were witnessing a long interval. They were discouraged. They had known better days—perhaps some mountaintop experiences. They were perplexed and could not understand the utter absence of the sense of God's presence. The writer comes along and shows them that this is nothing to despise. It is an opportunity to believe.

The great men of the Old Testament knew what it was to wait and live without the tangible evidence of God's blessing. They lived in reliance upon the faithfulness of God. How could they do that? Because they knew by virtue of His appearances to them that He could be trusted and believed. Though God hid His face for a season, they believed Him no less.

Although faith is not a New Testament innovation, it is a New Testament norm. The Christian life is a venture of believing God. Seeing is not believing. Believing is not seeing. Faith is an inner persuasion in those who live by the integrity and faithfulness of One whose manifested glory is worth waiting for.

In the meantime, faith accomplishes extraordinary things. How extraordinary? We turn now to the possibilities of faith.

Chapter Two

Faith and Works

Hebrews 11:2
For by it [faith] the elders obtained a good report.

Before the writer of Hebrews can illustrate the vast possibilities of faith, there is yet one more principle he wants to put before his readers. This principle is contained in the second verse of our chapter—the shortest verse, but in many ways the most important. The principle is this: Faith can do extraordinary things because it emancipates man's will to do what he previously could not do.

When our writer moves from his general description of faith in Hebrews 11:1 to the possibilities of faith in Hebrews 11:2, he spells out what is clearly a different function of faith. This new function of faith has actually been inherent in the Epistle to the Hebrews from early on. It began to emerge more perceptibly in the last part of chapter 10, particularly when he said, **"Cast not away therefore your confidence, which hath great recompense of reward" (v. 35).** The **"great recompense of reward"** was a promise of much more than what had been tied to faith up to then. Yet, the last thing which our writer would want us to do is forget that this is but a subsidiary effect of *believing God.*

What then was the primary aspect of faith considered in the preceding chapters of Hebrews? Salvation. That is what Hebrews is mostly about, and if we forget this as we examine this famous "faith chapter," we not only are unfair to the epistle itself, but leave ourselves most impoverished.

What is this new function of faith? It gives man freedom to be and to do what had been impossible for him prior to his own salvation. We have defined faith as *believing God*. Believing God, as opposed to falling away (Heb. 6:6) or drawing back (Heb. 10:39), assures one of one's interest in the mediatorial work of Jesus Christ. Believing God in the context of Christ's death and resurrection may be called *saving* faith. But the **"great recompense of reward"** of which the writer speaks in Hebrews 10:35 is much, much more than the assurance of salvation. By *continuing* to believe God, vast possibilities emerge that may be experienced right here on earth. Such experience may be called experimental faith.

"Experimental" Faith

Believing God, then, has two functions, one primary and the other subsidiary. Salvation is primary. The **"great recompense of reward"** is subsidiary. We may therefore speak of a saving faith and an experimental faith. Saving faith fits us for heaven; experimental faith fits us for earth. We are not ready to live until we are ready to die. Saving faith is the primary thing. Experimental faith is subsidiary.

The vast possibilities of faith described in Hebrews 11, then, are derived from experimental faith. Why call it "experimental"? Because it is a word that not only implies our experience but invites being tested at the empirical level. The marvel of faith is that it derives its strength from believing God without the evidence of things **"seen"** but produces works that are clearly visible to anybody who cares to observe.

Our writer describes experimental faith in Hebrews 11:2: **"For by it the elders obtained a good report." "This is what the ancients were commended for"** (NIV). The Greek word is *emarturethesan*, they **"received witness."** In other words, such witness or testimony came as a consequence of faith. Such faith is to be called experimental because it produced the kind of witness or result which could be *tested*. The writer to these Hebrew Christians claims that it was both tested and commended in the lives of the heroes he is describing.

There is in the study of theology what is known in Latin as the *ordo salutis* (order of salvation). It is not an unimportant matter, and the reader ought to try to grasp this. I should like to think that a subsidiary effect of reading my book will be a sharpening of your theological taste. I promise the reader that you will be rewarded if you will not only bear with this section but read it very carefully. Your own faith and understanding will be enriched if you can learn to think more theologically. Here is a good place to begin: the *ordo salutis*.

Raising the question of the "order of salvation" is somewhat like asking, "Which comes first—the chicken or the egg? Which comes first—faith or good works?" This issue was so important in the sixteenth century that the face of western civilization was radically altered as a result. Martin Luther was convinced that a man is justified by faith alone—faith without works—and that works came as a consequence of faith but contributed nothing to salvation. The issue then was the *ordo salutis*.

The question of order is at stake in Hebrews 11:2. If we fail to see the nature of faith, as it is indicated in this profound verse, all that follows in Hebrews 11 will mean much less to us. The writer simply says that by faith these people **"received witness" (Hebrews 11:4).** It is to be seen that faith produced the witness, not *vice versa*. The things which they did, then, are not what produced faith; what they did came as a *result* of their faith. Thus by believing and not seeing, a great many things happened. But their doing these things did not earn them salvation. They were not trying to earn salvation—the opposite is true—it is because they were already assured of God's integrity and faithfulness that they accomplished what they did.

Yet, it was experimental faith, not saving faith, which produced the commendation. Saving faith is intangible; experimental faith is tangible. Hebrews 11 contains one graphic demonstration after another of what one can do experimentally if one already feels accepted by God. God motivates men by accepting them. Our wills are not set free to explore unlimited possibilities through faith until our hearts are first persuaded that God loves us. In short, saving faith must come before experimental faith.

This discussion should help us to see how relevant a clear theological understanding is to the way we live the Christian life. Many Christians are in serious bondage because they have a confused, if not distorted, *ordo salutis* (even if they have never heard the expression). This is often due not only to a presently deficient spiritual diet but to the way they were introduced to Christianity in the first place. If a person is told that he must produce good works in order to know he is saved, he will always look to those works in an attempt to make his assurance firm. The sad fact is assurance never comes that way. For how can a person ever know if his works are at last sufficient to provide assurance?

True Assurance

Seeking assurance by works is but one step removed from seeking salvation by works. The writer of the Epistle to the Hebrews knows of neither. When he says that through faith the ancients obtained witness, he believes by now he has demonstrated that the question of salvation (or the assurance of it) has been replaced by the question, *What can faith do on earth?*

To put it another way: saving faith is seated in the heart; experimental faith is seated in the will. The point is that saving faith is being persuaded of what Jesus Christ our Mediator has done for us. Saving faith is not the "assent" of the mind but rather a heart persuasion that Jesus Christ has done all that was needed to accomplish our salvation (see Rom. 10:10). Saving faith, then, is basically passive—it is beholding—it is seeing what Christ *has done!* **"But we see Jesus" (Heb. 2:9).**

Experimental faith, on the other hand, is in the will—doing, and is active. It derives its motivation from its object: the Lord Jesus Christ. This **"seeing of the Son" (see John 6:40)** precipitates a certain activity in the one who has saving faith. Experimental faith gets its inspiration from saving faith. Saving faith therefore produces repentance (the admission "I was wrong"), sanctification and good works; it changes a person and makes him want to *do* things!

Faith's "Good Report"

Nevertheless, the believer may get discouraged and may need to be warned and encouraged to be truly motivated. This is precisely the writer's purpose in the Epistle to the Hebrews generally and chapter 11 particularly. He wants these Hebrew Christians to see not only the very real danger of what happens to those who **"draw back" (Heb. 10:38)** but also the unlimited possibilities for those who do not cast away their confidence. Thus having given his general description of faith in Hebrews 11:1, he shows the experimental nature of believing God: **"For by it the elders obtained a good report."**

The doctrine of salvation by grace through faith alone has always been vulnerable to the charge of "antinomianism" ("against law"), the belief that one may live lawlessly and still be a Christian. The Apostle Paul had to fight off this charge (Rom. 3:8). But, as Dr. D.M. Lloyd-Jones has said, unless our gospel is charged with antinomianism, it is not likely that it has truly been understood! For saving faith is beholding the Lord Jesus and knowing in our hearts that salvation is really ours by His work alone! We must be clear about this. It is not our task to go into any more detail concerning the earlier chapters of the Epistle to the Hebrews, but nothing is clearer from them than this wonderful fact: Jesus Christ our Mediator has accomplished by Himself all that was required of us.

So by saying that faith obtains a good report, our writer shows that what is at first saving faith should become an experimental faith. It is also his way of refuting the charge of antinomianism. He believes that we are fully emancipated to do good works because we are fully assured of our salvation. For the things which experimental faith demonstrates are not accomplished with a view to proving to ourselves that we are saved; we should already know that and be beyond the need for that assurance. Nevertheless, a good report gives proof that saving faith is there.

It is vitally important to understand this distinction. If one seeks to "do" certain things to prove to himself that he is saved, it betrays that he has never known full assurance of his salvation. It also shows that he has not been persuaded by **"seeing"** Jesus. Therefore, good works are not to be performed in order to prove salvation to ourselves. As long as one is working to prove salvation, his sanctification is selfishly motivated. A person is not truly emancipated to do good works until he has settled the issue of his own salvation. That matter must already have been dealt with before one can truly follow in the steps of the great personalities of Hebrews 11.

The **"good report,"** or commendation, is ultimately the consequence of not letting our right hand know what our left hand does, and yet it gives proof of true faith. Everybody can see it—it dazzles the world—it leaves them without any ground to condemn us, refutes the charge of antinomianism and demonstrates that one is so overwhelmed by the mercy of God that he cannot help but show it by his obedience. To get one glimpse of the integrity of God is to be persuaded of His faithfulness to keep us.

A sober reminder to be obedient might well be needed, for all of us tend to have a poor memory and can momentarily forget that we have been **"purged from our old sins" (II Pet. 1:9).** The good report, or witness of our faith, is therefore commanded in order that we may openly make our **"calling and election sure" (II Pet. 1:10).** But the only one who can do this is the one who knows already he has been given a most **"precious faith with us through the righteousness of God and our Saviour Jesus Christ" (II Pet. 1:1).**

Our writer tells us that the "elders," or ancients, received this commendation, that is, the men themselves. It is not merely this faith which gets the good report—the people do. It is not our faith that is commended—we are. Faith by itself is invisible and has no way of showing itself unaided. Faith is demonstrated by people. The world sees *us*—living personalities, real men and women who live in the real world like anybody else. It is not what we *believe* that matters to the world out there; it is what we *do*.

God often allows us to be commended for our actions—honored for doing merely what we ought to have done. Our writer freely puts these men on display and extols their virtues. He doesn't shy away from calling them by name. Yet, they did not do wonderful things because they thought they would someday be hailed as heroes. That never entered their minds. Any applause was only an unexpected byproduct of their lives of faith.

Chapter Three

Faith and Creation

Hebrews 11:3

Through faith we understand that the worlds were framed by the word of God, so that things which are seen were not made of things which do appear.

Sooner or later, every Christian in today's world encounters the question of creation versus evolution. Many want to believe in God and enjoy the venture of faith which the warriors of Hebrews 11 experienced, but prefer not to have to believe the Genesis account of creation. Indeed, there is a stigma associated with creation that many would like to side-step altogether.

The writer of the Epistle to the Hebrews will not let us do that. Early in this chapter on faith, he makes us face the question of creation by God *ex nihilo* (out of nothing). He will not let us move to the stalwarts of faith until we are clear on this matter of creation by God alone. There can hardly be a more relevant issue at the present time; it is undoubtedly one of the burning issues of our generation.

I suspect that the most common tool used by Satan today in his attack on historic Christianity is the theory of evolution. The masses now generally accept the theory of evolution uncritically, and many leading theologians and pastors have also capitulated to the spirit of the age and have made the Bible subsidiary to the latest scientific theory. It is my view that none of us should expect to experience faith as the Hebrews 11 heroes did, unless we also believe as they did concerning God's creation.

Every generation of Christianity has its own stigma by which the believer's faith is severely tested. For example, in the first generation of the church the stigma involved saying Jesus of Nazareth is the fulfillment of the Old Testament. Around the turn of the first century the critical issue came to be whether to praise Christ or Caesar. Entering the fourth century, the issue largely focused on the question of whether Jesus Christ was co-eternal and co-substantial with God Almighty. In Luther's day it was whether one was justified by faith or works.

These are just a few examples, but I could go on and on. The most hotly contested issue of any day involves something that is true, but which has become the minority view and branded as foolish. Athanasius was nearly alone in his day when he stood for the full deity of Jesus Christ. "The world is against you," they would say to Athanasius. "If the world is against Athanasius," he retorted, "then Athanasius is against the world."

We may think that our issue today is unprecedented in the seriousness of its threat to the Bible. We may fear that at long last the Bible will be dis-proved and Christianity made extinct. But *every* generation has its stigma by which the believer's faith is tested, and the issue is always that which appears to be the last blow to the Truth. Arguments emerge that had not been thought of before; evidence is put forward which seems completely new; issues coalesce that point to the impossibility of believing what the Apostles believed.

Today we are in a post-Newtonian era. The Apostle Peter, Athanasius, Luther and Calvin had no trouble believing in creation *ex nihilo*. "But this is a new day," it is often said, "and we must work out a faith that is consis-tent with modern science." The stigma of our generation, then, is to reject the theory of evolution and stand unflinchingly for creation by God: **"that things which are seen were not made of things which do appear."**

Thε Naturε of Faith

Behind the question of creation versus evolution is the very nature of faith itself. Will we believe God as a consequence of *what He has said*, putting His integrity on the line, or will our views be governed by so-called empirical proofs? Do we believe the Word of God for its own sake or pay homage to the empirical method before we can trust the Lord?

In other words, the issue is whether the *internal* witness of the Spirit has priority over the external witness of observable evidence. This issue is mirrored in the nature of saving faith. Are we Christians because we look at Christ directly, or must we wait for some other indication (e.g., repentance or good works) that we are saved? The gospel message says we can *know* we are accepted because of Jesus Christ and the internal witness of His Spirit (see Romans 8:16). But if we must look to our outward works for our assurance to be firm, then we are not enjoying a salvation by grace alone.

So also with the matter of believing Scripture: Do we believe the Bible is **"God-breathed"** because of an inner persuasion (the testimony of the Holy Spirit), or do we conclude that the Bible is true only in proportion to an external witness (e.g., archaeology or scientific verification)? The issue here is the evidence of nature versus the evidence of faith.

The stigma of our generation is to believe God's account of creation without the full empirical evidence. It is seldom pointed out to young people in school that the theory of evolution is just that—a theory. The search for evidence to prove evolution is largely an emotional reaction against some people's view of God. George Bernard Shaw summed it up: "If you can realize how insufferably the world was oppressed by the notion that everything that happened was an arbitrary personal act of an arbitrary personal God of dangerous, jealous and cruel personal character, you will understand how the world jumped at Darwin."

Still, Darwinism is yet to be proved. It is partly for this reason that there are actually *several* theories of evolution. Even after many years of scientific inquiry, the purported empirical evidence for any of these theories is inconclusive.

How we react to the stigma of *our* day provides a hint as to how we would have reacted to the stigma of a *former* day. Some of us are tempted to wish that we had lived in this or that era. Others might feel lucky that they were *not* living in a time of great persecution, as they fear they could not have stood it. There is a way to tell whether you could have stood it, and that is whether you are faithful to what is given to you now. It is as simple as that.

We are no weaker or stronger than the martyrs, no more and no less intelligent, and have by nature no more or less courage; neither are we naturally any more spiritual than any who lived in a previous age. Spirituality is not a natural endowment in the first place. Jesus said, **"He that is faithful in that which is least is faithful also in much" (Luke 16:10).** If we are faithful to the revelation God gives us in our day, it is sufficient proof that we would have been on the right side of the issues that mattered in a previous generation. The heroes of Hebrews 11 are those who accepted the stigma of their own day.

The attacks upon Christianity today come primarily from the culmination of two anti-God movements: Hegelian philosophy and Darwinism. Hegel's philosophy led to the emergence of Marxism and Higher Criticism of the Bible. These forces, combined with a denial of creation *ex nihilo*, have done more to undermine faith in the Bible than anything else has done in recent times. In the twentieth century, the church has largely succumbed to these trends. As a consequence, it is exceedingly difficult to find a churchman or theologian today who does not believe in some form of the theory of evolution. The conspiracy against the Bible has focused mainly on an undermining of the book of Genesis.

Created out of Nothing

The writer of Hebrews serves notice that he believes **"the worlds [ages] were framed by the word of God, so that things which are seen were not made of things which do appear."** This statement is worded very carefully and contains everything that is needed in order to show that one cannot hold to evolution and creation *ex nihilo* at the same time.

It is to be noted that the writer does not say that by faith we "prove" that the worlds were created by the word of God. This points to the mistake many are making. Some feel a need to spend a lot of time proving certain things in order to establish faith. I sometimes wonder if this need arises out of some embarrassment for the Bible.

I have a report in my files that describes the findings of a scientific laboratory which has proved the possibility of a virgin birth in higher mammals. This actually suggests to some that Jesus' miraculous birth is credible after all! However, it is not our task to "destigmatize" the faith by finding an analogy at the level of nature; rather, we should bear the stigma as we bear the cross of Jesus. We must be willing to be laughed at and still not rush to make our belief in the Bible credible to others.

Neither does the writer say that by "science" we understand. The mistake made by many is to assume that whatever science says is surely right. But what is science? It is a nebulous term that lacks an absolute consensus even as to its meaning. Many people listen to one scientist and think they have heard "science" speak! Scientists are people who have more and more knowledge about less and less. We forget that they are quite human and therefore fallible. Today nearly all of them specialize to such an extent that they are often ignorant of what is going on outside their own field. Sadly, the world is largely unaware of a rising number of scientists (some Christian, some nonchristian) who do not believe in evolution at all.

The writer says it is **"through faith"** that we understand. In other words, understanding comes as we *believe God.* **"The fear of the Lord is the beginning of wisdom: and the knowledge of the holy is understanding" (Proverbs 9:10).** Believing God brings a breakthrough to knowledge and understanding.

Because we believe God, then, we understand that He spoke the universe into existence. In a hundred years it may be that more and more scientists will believe this even by empirical knowledge. This should not surprise us. For after all, empirical knowledge has dismally failed to make their evolutionary theory more than just a theory. One wonders how *far behind* science generally is as a result of scientists' uncritical acceptance of evolutionary thinking. And *yet if the majority of scientists were to deny evolution, this should not be our reason for accepting the biblical account any more quickly. For it is by "faith" that we believe in creation in the first place.*

Hebrews 11:3 says it is by faith that **"we"** understand. Though **"we"** understand, others may not. But who are **"we"**? The company of believers. The world may not understand. Many scientists may not understand. But **"we"** do—we who are the family of God—because creation really is a family secret. It is something we understand by faith. It was never meant to be understood by those outside the family. It is not a case of believing in creation and then being adopted into the family; rather, we are adopted into the family and then we discover the truth.

One of the problems some Christians create for themselves is that they get defensive about a family secret, and then it becomes a family scandal. The Christian should never apologize for what has been revealed by the Holy Spirit, regardless of whether those outside the family ever come to affirm the same thing.

Why I Believe

Apart from my conviction that God's Word is faithful and true, if you were to ask why I believe that He created time and space out of nothing, I would answer: Because of the power God has displayed in my own life. When I consider what God has done for me, I find Genesis the easiest book in the world to understand. If God can save me, He can save anybody. If God can save you, He can save anybody. If God can save any of us, He can do *anything*.

By faith, then, we understand. What precisely is it that we understand? That the things which **"appear"**—time and space and matter—were not made of things that already existed. This **"out of nothing"** activity of God is the essence of creation. Through faith we understand that time, space and matter were brought into being by the word—the command—of God. Things which are *there* were *put there* from *nothing* by the voice of God.

"And God said, 'Let there be light: and there was light'" (Genesis 1:3). This of course totally contradicts pantheism, the view that everything is God—flowers, birds, humans and all of nature. Pantheism asserts that nature is God because it assumes the eternity of matter, that there has *always* been time and space and matter. The writer of Hebrews was no pantheist.

Neither was he upholding *panentheism*—the concept that everything is *in* God. This was Paul Tillich's position, a supposed mediating position between pantheism and theism. Many have followed him, for here they found what appeared to be a halfway point between atheism and Christianity. In the words of Harvey Cox, Tillich is "the indispensable comforter of those who grew up in a faith they can no longer believe."

Those who are attracted to panentheism (even though they may never have heard of the term) generally subscribe to the idea of theistic evolution. Some even believe they can hold to creation *ex nihilo* and evolution at the same time. Their view is that evolution was merely God's way of bringing things to what they are today.

Mixing God and Evolution

Those who subscribe to theistic evolution take their cue not from Scripture but from nature and "science." They believe that the external witness has priority over the internal witness. They assume that since so many scientists believe in evolution, there must be something to it. So they begin with the assumption that evolution is probably true—but so is the Bible, at least up to a point. And yet our writer tells us that what is seen at the level of nature was not made out of what is visible. Any view of evolution takes it for granted that what now appears has *evolved* to its present state from what already existed.

Superimposing the name of God upon a system of thought that was never intended to align with His inspired Word is a futile endeavor. The things that are **"seen"** (Greek *phainomenon,* **"what is being seen"**) **"were not made"** (Greek *gegonenai,* **"brought into being"**) by **"things which do appear"** (Greek *blepomenon,* **"what is visible"**). If the writer of Hebrews had seen civilization 1900 years later and wished to make a statement that would categorically refute any view of evolution, he could not have worded it better.

To take one's cue from nature is to assume the reliability of nature. But nature is cursed (Genesis 3:17) and has consequently ceased to be a reliable mirror by which to view the age of the world or the way in which things came into being. It is not surprising, then, that "science" is always changing. A scientific dictionary is out of date in less than ten years, and yet theologians keep running after modern science. What science claims to be true today, theology will probably say tomorrow. What a pity that this is so! Theology ought to set the pace and command scientists to respect the Most High God.

Many scientists have sufficient integrity to admit their own inconsistencies. One prominent scientist recently pointed out that evolutionists have continually failed to admit that the theory of evolution flies directly in the face of some of the most established laws in the scientific world. Some of the foundations which had been assumed are now crumbling. We should not be surprised at this, but neither should we necessarily be encouraged. For it is *by faith* that we understand!

When we affirm creation **"out of nothing,"** we are actually affirming what is perhaps the deepest thing that can be said about God—that He always was. This means, moreover, that He was not always creating. The panentheistic view is that God is Creator because it is His essential nature to create, that He has always been creating. It follows, if that is true, that there is no such thing as a "beginning" of time or of space and matter. But one of the most profound things we can say about God is that creation had a "beginning"—that "before" then there was *nothing but God!*

To believe this at the present time, however, is to be outnumbered and often scoffed at. Yet if it were not this issue, there would be another that would be just as open to mockery. For every generation has its own stigma by which the believer is tested. We must not side-step this bearing of the cross or try to "destigmatize" the faith. If we don't accept the stigma, we cannot expect to follow in the steps of the giants of the faith described in Hebrews 11, men and women who through faith understood that **"the worlds were framed by the word of God."**

Chapter Four

CAIN AND ABEL

Hebrews 11:4

By faith Abel offered unto God a more excellent sacrifice than Cain, by which he obtained witness that he was righteous, God testifying of his gifts: and by it he being dead yet speaketh.

The writer to the Hebrews not only draws heavily on the Book of Genesis to demonstrate his view that faith is not a New Testament innovation, but he also assumes its historicity. It is important that such an assumption is our own if we are ever to approach the experience of faith that characterized the great men of Hebrews 11.

One of the follies to be found in the modern church is that so many want to expound the New Testament without holding to the same convictions concerning the Old Testament to which the New Testament writers were committed. It is my own view that the church will never again be the salt of the earth God intends until it recovers its persuasion concerning the cosmological reliability and the anthropological accuracy of the Book of Genesis.

The writer of Hebrews believes that the fall of man occurred in history and that the Garden of Eden was a place on the map. However, instead of discussing the emergence of sin in Eden's garden, he moves instead from the subject of creation (v. 3) to the account of Cain and Abel. Why does he do this? And what would make him apparently think of Abel as the first man of faith in human history? Why didn't the writer begin with Enoch, the man of whom it is explicitly stated that he walked with God? Or why didn't he begin with Adam?

Though we may be surprised to find Abel at the very beginning of this "Hall of Fame of Faith," it is clear that the writer could not have begun with Adam. Adam was not a man of faith. Adam was a man of unbelief. Adam did not believe God. God told him the truth. The devil approached Eve through the serpent: **"Yea, hath God said, Ye shall not eat of every tree of the garden?"** The devil's approach in the Garden of Eden was what it has consistently been ever since—to get men to doubt God's Word.

The devil succeeded with Eve, for she succumbed to doubt. Adam followed, so we have in our first parents the embodiment of unbelief. They are the disgrace of the whole family of God, the scandal of the human race. This is why the writer of Hebrews bypassed the subject of man's fall, choosing instead to jump immediately from the subject of creation to the positive role models of faith.

The writer to the Hebrews knew that Abel, the offspring of Adam and Eve, could not have done what he did apart from faith. Here was a man who offered to God a sacrifice of blood. He is said to have **"obtained witness that he was righteous" (Hebrews 11:4).** The obvious question then is this: How did Abel know he should bring a sacrifice of blood? There are two possibilities. One is that he was taught to do so by his parents. After Adam and Eve sinned we are told that God gave them garments made of animal skins (Gen. 3:21). This provision required the shedding of blood, and it constituted the beginning of the Old Testament sacrificial system.

Although Adam and Eve were hardly the perfect parents or perfect examples, it is quite likely that Cain and Abel were taught to offer sacrifices of blood. The other possibility is that God Himself spoke to Cain and Abel. Again and again God communicated with people in the Old Testament, and surely the voice of the Spirit would have been sufficient to instruct Cain and Abel on such matters as blood sacrifices. It took no more faith for them to believe the Spirit than it does for us to believe the Scriptures. God gives sufficient witness to every generation.

CAIN AND ABEL   33

An Acceptable Offering

God offered His grace equally to both Cain and Abel. For Abel's offering was not a leap in the dark. He didn't consider it a gamble that a sacrificial offering of blood might please God. Abel did what he did because he believed God. But what about Cain? Cain opted for nature; he chose to follow his conscience. Cain thought that if his conscience was appeased through nature, he would do even better than what God commanded.

Samuel's rebuke to King Saul, who thought he had a better idea than that of taking God's command literally, would have applied equally as well to Cain: **"To obey is better than sacrifice" (I Samuel 15:22).** Cain's sin has been repeated countless times. We sometimes think we are going to impress God by doing this or that; but God only wants us to believe Him.

Abel believed God. But Cain wanted to do one better and followed the course of nature: he offered the fruit of the cursed ground. We may ask, "Why did not God accept Cain's offering? After all, must it have been an animal sacrifice?" I believe the answer can be found in the Book of Genesis itself without having to move on to Leviticus, in which we learn that **"without the shedding of blood there is no remission" (Lev. 17:11 and Heb. 9:22).** Look at the creation story. Cain's offering—the fruit of the ground—corresponded to the third day of creation. **"And God said, Let the earth bring forth grass, the herb yielding seed, and the fruit tree yielding fruit after his kind, whose seed is in itself, upon the earth: and it was so" (Gen. 1:11).**

Abel's offering, however, corresponds to the sixth day of creation (Gen. 1:24-31) in which both animals and man were created. Abel's offering prefigured atonement by substitution: what God required was not vegetation substituting for man but a slain animal substituting for man. Vegetation is not an analogy to man, but a beast is. Whether it be a lamb, a goat or a bull, a beast is the nearest likeness to man, and both were created on the same day. God always demanded a sacrifice of blood throughout the Old Testament.

But the wonder of wonders is in the new covenant, which was not a case of vegetation substituting for sinful man or even beasts substituting for sinful man. Instead, God became man and was the perfect man substituting for sinful man. When God Himself became man, He who knew no sin was **"made sin"** for us, **"that we might be made the righteousness of God in him"** (II Cor. 5:21).

Put simply: Cain did not wish to accept God's prescribed method of worship. He preferred to bring the labors of his own hands. He tried to appease his conscience by works. Yet Cain had equal opportunity to do as his brother did. **"And the Lord said unto Cain, Why art thou wroth? and why is thy countenance fallen? If thou doest well, shalt thou not be accepted? and if thou doest not well, sin lieth at the door"** (Gen. 4:6-7). Thus, before God rejected Cain entirely, He gave him a second warning. It was obvious that what God was wanting was precisely what Abel had brought. So God in effect said to Cain, "If you do the same thing, you too will be accepted." But Cain chose not to accept God's provision.

What Abel did, he did **"by faith."** He believed God. He proved it by offering a **"more excellent sacrifice"** than Cain. What emerges, then, is that this man Cain prefigures those who are reprobate, or apostate, as opposed to God's elect. Yet this should also help us to see once and for all that those who are damned are condemned by their own sins, and those who are justified are saved by a righteousness outside themselves. The one who is justified can take no credit for it; the one who is damned can only blame himself. This we learn from the Genesis account of Cain and Abel.

Cain thus becomes an example of apostasy—that is drawing back in the face of a mediator. **"If we sin wilfully after that we have received the knowledge of the truth, there remaineth no more sacrifice for sins"** (Heb. 10:26). Cain was the first reprobate in human history.

But Abel, the first man of faith, **"obtained witness"** that **"he"** was righteous. It is not that what Abel did was righteous in itself—it is that he was declared righteous. If what he *did* is what was righteous, then faith becomes a work, but we are told that *Abel* was righteous. God does not accept our works as meriting anything towards being justified—he accepts *us*. He is not asking us to do things in order to be justified, for all that we can do prior to faith can but be described as filthy in His sight (see Isa. 64:6). God does not favorably regard the works we did prior to our justification. There is no preparation for justification. When we come to God through His Son, we are accepted in our persons, for *we* are considered righteous.

Abel's Gifts

Did Abel know that he was righteous? Yes, he did. How did he know? Abel had the greatest witness of all: *God* testified of his gifts (v. 4). Could anybody desire a greater witness than that? How then do *we* know that we are accepted? In the same way: God testifies that we are justified and that we are adopted into His family.

But some may well ask, "How can a person know that God witnesses to the fact of their salvation?" The answer relates to the question, What is our "gift"? If you are struggling to gain assurance, struggling to know that God loves you and has accepted you, I must ask you this question: What is your "gift"? For the writer of Hebrews tells us that Abel obtained witness that he was righteous by God testifying of his "gifts."

What "gift" are *you* bringing to God? Are you still striving to gain His favor and acceptance by what you do? Have you promised to start attending church more? Perhaps you have decided to give God your tithes or to study your Bible more. Are these the types of gifts you are bringing to Him? Are you still trying to be accepted through nature, through whatever "vegetation" you can cultivate, or through conscience? Or can you say:

Nothing in my hand I bring,

Simply to Thy cross I cling?

How do you know you are accepted? The answer is Christ. Do you need more than that? Surely not. You are accepted, then. But not by what you do. What is our gift? Christ. "Nothing in my hand I bring." When you are persuaded that God has respect only for the sacrifice of His Son and that you have no other plea but Christ, you already have the witness. Not to believe the witness is not to believe God. **"For God so loved the world that He gave His only begotten Son, that whosoever believeth in Him should not perish, but have everlasting life" (John 3:16).**

The account of Cain and Abel, however, has a very sad ending. Just as faith has its confirmation, so does unbelief have its confirmation. Faith obtains a good report. Unbelief obtains a bad report. For those who try to purify their consciences by their own works end up with greater sin than ever. Those whose consciences are purified by the blood of Christ have the good report. The irony is that those who follow conscience and do things their own way never get a good conscience.

The fact is that when we opt for our natural reasoning and self-effort, we set ourselves up to do the unthinkable. We may feel most indignant over the senseless crimes we read about in the newspaper or see on television. You may say, "I would never do a thing like that." If your conscience is not made pure by the blood of Christ, do not ever say that. For if you should bypass God's way of worship—through the sacrifice of His Son—and opt to follow the course of what seems natural to you, you set yourself up for even the most heinous kind of sin.

"And it came to pass, when they were in the field, that Cain rose up against Abel his brother, and slew him" (Gen. 4:8). We are told that Abel's blood cried up from the ground, the very thing the writer to the Hebrews meant when he said that Abel, being dead, **"yet speaketh"** **(Hebrews 11:4).** Cain, who refused to dignify the grace that was offered him, was left utterly to himself. Cain had only himself—his unbridled, carnal heart. This is all that men have when they follow their own hearts rather than plead nothing but the merit, the name and the shed blood of God's only Son. When they reject the only thing that can help them, they open the floodgates of their depraved nature. From then on, anything is possible.

These words, **"He being dead, yet speaketh,"** demonstrate that God often vindicates His own after death. Cain thought that he had eliminated the only witness who could testify against him. But he was wrong. **"Be sure your sin will find you out"** (Num. 32:23). God has a way of uncovering sin and evil despite one's most ingenious way of covering it. God can expose us and find us out as He did Jonah. **"He that covereth his sins shall not prosper: but whoso confesseth and forsaketh them shall have mercy"** (Prov. 28:13).

When the writer to the Hebrews brought the faith of Abel to this list of men of **"good report,"** he gave us the one example of *saving* faith in Hebrews 11. For what follows are men of *experimental* faith. Saving faith must come before experimental faith, and yet experimental faith proves that one has saving faith indeed. However, men are not saved by their experience; what they do by faith shows the unlimited possibilities of one who has grasped the power of believing God.

The faith of Abel is a demonstration that God is pleased with Abel apart from his doing anything at all. Abel did not live long enough to do anything once Cain's jealousy took hold. The glory of Abel's faith is that *he himself* was seen as righteous. Had Abel lived, he no doubt would have demonstrated experimental faith even as the thief on the cross (Luke 23:39-43) would have done. But it is no small comfort to know that God does not grant us entrance into heaven by what we do in any case.

The experimental faith that is demonstrated in the following verses shows the motivating force in those who are assured that there *is* a heaven and that they are indeed going there!

Chapter Five

ENOCH

Hebrews 11:5

By faith Enoch was translated that he should not see death; and was not found, because God had translated him: for before his translation he had this testimony, that he pleased God.

Enoch is one of the least spectacular and yet one of the most godly men in the Old Testament. Eight verses in the Bible tell us all we directly know about him: six verses from Genesis 5:18-24; Jude 14 and Hebrews 11:5. It would seem that the writer to the Hebrews had the Book of Genesis in front of him as he was accumulating Old Testament evidence to show that the notion of faith is nothing new. Thus when he came to Enoch in Genesis 5, he dipped his pen in ink to add Enoch to the list of those who obtained a good report **"by faith."**

Very little indeed is known about this man Enoch, and yet what we do know about him is sufficient to set him apart from all others in his own generation. What we know about Enoch is this: who his father was (Jared); that his father outlived Enoch by 435 years; that Enoch was the father of Methuselah, the oldest man in the Bible (living 969 years); that Enoch himself **"walked with God"**; that at the age of 365 he disappeared, **"for God took him"**; and that during his life time he prophesied of the second coming of Jesus (Jude 14).

The writer of Hebrews might have missed Enoch, but I suspect that the statement **"Enoch walked with God; and he was not; for God took him" (Genesis 5:24)** arrested his attention. The writer knew that Enoch could not have achieved this apart from faith. We know nothing about Enoch's father; perhaps Jared was made known by his son. **"A wise son maketh a glad father" (Prov. 10:1),** and perhaps Jared had much to talk about during the 435 years in which he survived the disappearance of his son. Enoch disappeared in middle age (according to the life expectancy in those days); but as he walked with God during his comparatively short life on earth, he was given a clear revelation of not the first but the second coming of Jesus. Apparently Enoch unintentionally spawned a sort of tradition in his name and became a legendary figure in Israel. He was referred to in the Apocrypha (Wisdom of Solomon 4:10 and Ecclesiasticus 44:6), and Jude quotes from the Book of Enoch 1:9.

Walking with God—Without Fanfare

That which set Enoch apart from the rest of his generation was his sudden disappearance, and yet there was something that lay behind that disappearance in which his real secret is to be found: Enoch **"walked with God."** Yet surely this man Enoch was not the man who would be voted by his contemporaries as the man "most likely to be remembered in history"!

Are you aware that the writer to the Hebrews passed by another Enoch as he referred to the Book of Genesis for source material? There was an Enoch before our own Enoch of this chapter, and this other Enoch was a contemporary of our Enoch. The other Enoch was a son of Cain (Gen. 4:17), and without doubt Enoch the son of Cain was the more spectacular by contemporary standards. The first city mentioned in the Bible was named after Enoch the son of Cain. How many of us have had a city built in our name?

It is likely that if you had been living in Enoch's day and had been asked to predict which Enoch would have become best known in history, you would have confidently picked the man after whom a city was named. Surely you would have anticipated that the Enoch so well known in his own day would be the one to be remembered in history. But chances are you were not even aware of this other Enoch until this moment.

The Enoch who is subject of this chapter is well known today, but probably was largely unnoticed in his own day. Our Enoch did not have a city named after him; we do not read that he had a noble heritage or that he had great gifts; there is no hint that he had a gift of oratory or that he had a great personality, much less that he was a charismatic leader. We do not read that he had any fame at all in his own day. The chances are that he was not noticed until he was missed! **"Who hath despised the day of small things?" (Zech. 4:10).** His genius was this: He walked with God.

Consider the people you hear so much about at the present time, such as those you see on television. Consider the movie stars, the best-selling authors, the noisy politicians. The question is, will posterity even recall them? Even twenty years from now? It is quite likely that Enoch the city, not the Enoch who walked with God, was the talk of that generation.

I recall most vividly a feeling I endured in my high school years in Ashland, Kentucky. I seldom saw my name in the high school newspaper or the annual yearbook, much less was I alongside those who were voted "most likely to succeed." Such lack of notice gave me a deep inferiority complex. But a couple of years ago I was in my home town and inquired about certain persons. One cannot imagine the shock when I learned that many of those "most promising" students have turned out to be awful tragedies in life.

I give the above illustration for the encouragement of any young person or student who might read these lines. I know the pressure of wanting to be accepted. I know the feeling of wanting to be successful and to be liked. I know the experience of fear that comes from being "different" because of religious convictions. I know what it is to be ignored because one is not a part of the "crowd." But I make you a promise, and you may hold me to it: five years from now (which may seem long to you, but I assure you, it is not!) you will have an altogether different perspective regarding the "crowd" that now occupies so much of your attention.

That which seems so important to you now will be almost meaningless in a short period of time. I will tell you what counts and what matters: to walk with God. Learn not to succumb to the pressures of your age. Young people, learn to say "NO." Keep your purity and refuse to give in to what you think those of the opposite sex want. Prove your Christianity by standing tall under the pressures of temptation.

The writer to the Hebrews passed over the first Enoch. But that is not all whom the writer passed by. What do you know about Jabal, Jubal and Tubalcain? You don't know about them? Let me tell you about them. Jabal, Jubal and Tubalcain were the great-great-great-great-grandchildren of Cain. Jabal was the father of the construction business; Jubal was the father of music; and Tubalcain was the father of the hardware business and also of sculpturing.

In these three men one may see the beginnings of the arts and sciences. With these three there thus emerges more fully the doctrine of common grace. These men were blessed with particular gifts and talents. They had special abilities and knowledge. Do not underestimate this. Thank God for this. Thank God for the builders, farmers, musicians, businessmen and artists. Thank God for the natural pursuits which have brought us medical advancements, electricity and the like. Yet when the writer to the Hebrews was looking for the men of faith in the Old Testament, he passed over these three men, although they were famous in their own day. Many famous men are not Christians. There are many famous people who are either buried or honored in Westminster Abbey, but I would not want to stand in their shoes in the Judgment. The contributions of great men are to be appreciated; otherwise Jabal, Jubal and Tubalcain would not get special mention in the Book of Genesis. But there is a kind of grace far more important than common grace. Though all men have a measure of common grace, **"all men have not faith"** (II Thess. 3:2).

Enoch was not a spectacular man, but he walked with God. The writer to the Hebrews adds that Enoch **"pleased God."** We are not told that Enoch pleased his friends or his family, for that is sometimes hard to do. We are told that he pleased God, and that is something any of us can do-- by faith.

You may ask: "What did Enoch believe? What did God say to him? If faith is believing God, what was it to which Enoch was faithful?" The writer to the Hebrews tells us, **"By faith Enoch was translated that he should not see death."** God promised Enoch that he would not die; otherwise, this verse makes no sense. Enoch was not translated in order to believe;

obviously he believed first. He believed he would not see death, and his faith achieved this translation into heaven without death.

You may ask: "What precedent was there for believing that God would reveal such a thing to Enoch?" I answer: God does not need a precedent to be guided by, neither does He have to do anything twice. But why did the Lord translate Enoch into heaven without his having to pass through death's chilly waters? I offer two reasons. First, God did it for Enoch's own sake. God delights in communicating Himself to us and deals singularly with us—as though there were no one else to love. **"He that spared not His own Son, but delivered Him up for us all, how shall He not with Him also freely give us all things?" (Rom. 8:32).**

Second, God did it for the sake of Enoch's own generation. It served as a reminder to that generation that there was something better to come, a reminder that life in the here and now is not all there is—there is more. There is something beyond the realm and level of nature. The natural world is *not* all there is. Enoch's sudden disappearance was a vindication of this truth. Not only was it a witness to his own generation, it also served as a warning of how grave and serious Adam's sin was. This translation of Enoch into heaven was the indication to all living what Adam would have obtained had he not sinned.

Enoch believed God, and God took him. Moreover, believing God in Enoch's day was no easier than in our day. There is not the remotest truth in the notion that it was easier to believe in God or believe His Word in a previous generation. Every generation has its stigma by which the believer's earnestness is tested. Every generation has its obstacle which faith must overcome. Every believer of each generation is sooner or later placed in the dilemma of looking like a fool, a simpleton, if he believes the Lord.

Obstacles to Enoch's Faith

There were two obstacles to faith in Enoch's day which might have aborted his walk with God. The first is the prosperity of Cain's family. Here was a stigma to be faced, for Jabal, Jubal and Tubalcain were symbols of prosperity and contemporary fame. Yet there is not the slightest indication that they were believers. We often hear it said, "If there is a God, why do wicked men prosper?" This is a question that every generation in human history has had to face. **"Fret not thyself because of evildoers, neither be thou envious against the workers of iniquity" (Psalm 37:1).** Why go on believing God when those who do not believe seem better off materially?

Enoch's second obstacle was this: He had been told he would not die, but he had to watch everyone around him dying. Do you realize that Enoch witnessed the death of Adam, that Enoch was alive when Adam died? Adam lived 930 years, and then Genesis 5:5 records for the first time the ultimate consequence of Adam's sin: **"and he died."** After Adam died, others died—one patriarch after another. There was not any precedent for believing that Enoch would not see death.

One of the essential ingredients of faith is that God tests us in such a manner that there is no exact precedent for our own situation or trial. And yet faith must be like this, or there would be a natural basis for making faith solid. God comes to every individual in such a manner as to wipe out all precedents, that there may be nothing for us to do but to believe God.

There is, however, one thing which many of us have in common with Enoch. Many of us are in some sense products of the Great Reformation of the sixteenth century, if not also the Great Awakening of the eighteenth century. Enoch was a product of the first great awakening in the history of the world.

This first great awakening is recorded in Genesis 4:26: **"Then began men to call upon the name of the Lord."** This was the first time men grasped the name of God and called on Him. Jonathan Edwards in *History of the Work of Redemption* pauses long at this point and shows that Enoch was a product of this apparent revival. It tells us something of the atmosphere that precipitated Enoch's walk with God. But he could not lean on that awakening; he had to move on and believe God in his own day.

Enoch pleased God and knew that he pleased Him. How did he know that he pleased God? The answer is: God told him so. For **"before his translation he had this testimony [witness], that he pleased God."** This should not surprise us. John tells us that the one who believes in the Son **"hath the witness in himself" (I John 5:10).**

You may say, "But it is one thing to believe on Christ and quite another to have Enoch's faith, which was in the Old Testament." Yet, do not forget that Enoch prophesied that the Lord Jesus Christ should come with ten thousands of his saints (Jude 14). We are dealing with a man who walked so close to God that he was elevated to a spiritual realm that lost all sense of time. Enoch's faith was tied to the Lord Jesus Christ. Enoch pleased God and knew it.

Do you please God? If you do not know, the reason is this—it's because you are trying to please God by your works. Your works will never bring about the knowledge that you please Him. We are not told that Enoch was translated **"by works,"** but rather that it was "by faith." If you want to please Him, believe Him.

Chapter Six

PLEASING GOD

Hebrews 11:6

But without faith it is impossible to please Him: for he that cometh to God must believe that He is, and that He is a rewarder of them that diligently seek Him.

Hebrews 11:6 includes what is perhaps the most crucial point the writer to the Hebrews will make in the entire epistle. This verse will give someone a clear indication as to whether or not he is even a Christian. The writer seems to have the Book of Genesis in front of him as he proceeds to list the heroes of faith, and he now wishes to make an essential point before moving on to his next example. If we do not grasp this point, it is unlikely that we will comprehend what the writer says about faith later on. Without understanding the principles behind this verse, we run the risk of forgetting why Hebrews 11 was given to us in the first place.

Why do we have this magnificent eleventh chapter of the Epistle to the Hebrews? It is mainly to show that (1) faith obtains a good report; (2) faith is believing God without the empirical proof; and (3) faith is the only guarantee against apostasy. We must remember that the writer was addressing only a remnant of Hebrew Christians, for many had already fallen away. The writer had given a rationale for such apostasy, but also gave an infallible hope that such a defection need not characterize the rest of us.

We may *know* that we will not fall as some have done. The ground of apostasy was the rejection of Christ the Mediator; the ground of assurance is to honor Christ the Mediator. We may therefore know that we will not fall away because we keep our eyes upon the Mediator. This Mediator has been revealed to us by way of *promise*—the way God always comes to men.

Before proceeding any further, the writer wants to make sure that we have understood this fundamental principle of God's dealings with men: **"without faith it is impossible to please God."** This verse is obviously a continuation of the verse which describes Enoch's faith, and it is another confirmation that it was faith by which Enoch pleased God. The writer wants to cut away any possibility that there is something we can do prior to faith that pleases God. When the writer claims that **"without faith it is impossible to please God,"** he rules out any preparation for grace on man's part prior to faith. We therefore conclude that what may be produced without faith cannot please God.

This is a humbling matter. It does indeed tell us whether we are Christians, for if we are trying to please God by our own efforts, we stand condemned by Hebrews 11:6. There are countless admirable things which we may produce without faith. Take repentance, for example. Those who had fallen away (Heb. 6:4-6) had been characterized partly by repentance. It was **"repentance"** particularly to which they cannot be renewed—which indicates that they once had experienced it.

Repentance is one ingredient in experimental faith, but any change of life preceding saving faith is of no value. Whereas the great men in this eleventh chapter of Hebrews experienced everything from a change of life to extreme suffering, all experimental faith is but the consequence of believing God.

Believing that God *Is*

We must recognize this fundamental assumption of the writer: that believing God is the primary thing; all else that may go before faith is useless. Such an assumption shows the folly of a popular teaching, "Show God that you mean business." According to the writer to the Hebrews, such talk is nonsense and is but fleshly thinking. What is more foolish than trying to "show God" something? The flesh wants to show God something; the Spirit shows us something.

There are those who teach that a prerequisite to faith is the removal of "every known sin." The poor soul who falls prey to this is usually the one who never has assurance of his salvation, for he is constantly aware of yet one more defect that delays faith. To the person who thinks repentance must come before faith in the order of salvation, there is the endless, nagging concern, "Have I repented enough?"

The writer to the Hebrews wants us **"to believe that *God is*."** *This* is where we begin. We are not in a position to repent or enjoy experimental faith until we have believed God! God accepts us as we are that we might do things; we do not do things in order to be accepted. As long as we keep looking to ourselves and substituting what we have done for what Christ has done, we will never follow in the steps of these great men of Hebrews 11. The only prerequisite to faith is the promise of God; either we believe it or we do not.

True faith always includes these inseparable attributes: (1) believing that God is *and* (2) believing that He is a rewarder of those who diligently seek Him. At the bottom of this discussion is this-- coming to God. When we come to God we do so empty-handed.

In my hand no price I bring;

Simply to Thy cross I cling.

The awareness that God *is* comes to man as a shock. Paul Tillich would speak of the "ontological shock," a concept he borrowed from Martin Heidegger. Why is there something and not nothing? Of course Tillich's use of the ontological shock is utterly man-centered. Ontology is the philosophy of being—"to be or not to be, that is the question." It is an ontological shock when I am aware that *I am*—that I am in a body that moves and that I can make my body move. But far greater than the ontological shock is the *theological* shock—that *God* is, that I am His creation, that I have a soul, and that I have sinned against Him. The theological shock is also the realization that there is a hell and that the natural realm of existence is not all there is.

When I am able to see God in this light, it does not enter my mind to come to Him in my own name or on the basis of what I have done. Such a God is so overwhelming and terrible that I know in my heart of hearts that I need His mercy. I know at once I need a Mediator—just by the realization that God is!

But the second realization in faith is that God will not reject me, for He is a rewarder of those who diligently seek Him. The thrust of contemporary theology (as exemplified in the thinking of Tillich) is anthropological—man-centered. Most modern theology never really moves beyond man. However, the assumption of the writer to the Hebrews is not only that we believe that God is, *but also* that He is a rewarder of those who diligently seek Him. I know conclusively that I am accepted, not rejected. This is true faith. It is neither my projection nor a vain conjecture. An essential part of faith is realizing that God has integrity, that He is there before me, that He listens when I talk to Him, and that He will keep His word to me. True faith is not merely to believe that He is, but that He *rewards*—He responds, He shows Himself, He answers!

To this principle the writer to the Hebrews appends a qualifying note—God rewards those who **"diligently seek Him."** He does not reward us merely because we believe that He is. Even the devils believe that much (James 2:19). Neither does God reward us merely because we *believe* that He is **"a rewarder."** The demons believe and even tremble, but the demons cannot diligently seek God! If fact, why would *anybody* want to diligently seek God? For this one reason—we have become persuaded of His integrity and of His promise.

The writer to the Hebrews wants to establish the point that faith perseveres. It stands the test of time. It is a lifetime of coming to God despite those who may draw back. The writer not only wants to show the persevering nature of faith, but also the autonomy of faith—that you face the stigma of your generation by yourself. You believe God if nobody else does. It may seem easy to believe if there are many people around you who believe in God, but that might be nothing more than a natural prop to your faith.

THE AUTONOMY OF OUR FAITH

As a child I was brought up in a church that gave an "altar call" (invitation or appeal) at the close of every sermon. With children especially there is a bandwagon effect, for if there should be a whole row of us and one quite popular lad should "go forward," everybody else would follow. This is anything but an autonomous faith. These Hebrew Christians had a wonderful opportunity to prove their faith, for many of their friends were defecting from the faith right and left. To persevere in the face of this was a sign of true faith.

In this connection it must be said that one of the sadder moments in the history of Christian evangelism has been the introduction of celebrities into evangelistic campaigns. However sincere the motives may be that lie behind the football player, the movie star or the beauty queen who gives a testimony for the Lord, this is but an unconscious conspiracy to destigmatize the faith. Whatever else it does, it undermines the autonomy of faith. If I become a Christian because of the feeling that says, "If a person of such stature or fame has become a Christian, then perhaps it won't be so bad if I do," I betray that my ultimate concern is people and not God. Jesus asked, **"How can ye believe, which receive honor one of another, and seek not the honor that cometh from God only?" (John 5:44)**

Such autonomy not only relates to one's initiation into the Christian faith by conversion, but also to the manner in which one grows in knowledge and grace. If a profession of faith has a weak foundation when it is due to being impressed with the personality or prestige of a particular person, so is it dangerous to blindly receive doctrine *after* one has become a Christian. For example, a theological principle ought not to be received merely because it is held to by someone of renown. The writer to the Hebrews is trying to get us to believe God if nobody else does and to believe His Word if nobody else does.

If our faith is an autonomous faith, we will not be afraid to be tested along the way. We will pass the test every time because the object of faith is God Himself. We believe Him. We believe His Word. We therefore are not afraid to examine ourselves. One big problem with many today is that they have never examined themselves, especially those who have been brought up in the church. They may have been spoon-fed certain truths all their lives, but they have never bothered to look at themselves objectively or critically examine what they believe. Autonomous faith is not easily threatened, neither does it operate by a spirit of fear that forbids looking at oneself critically.

If you have come to question your own conversion or the manner in which you made your own profession of faith, there is a simple test for you: What is your response to the gospel now? If your profession was largely motivated by another's persuasion, or by tragedy that drove you to the church, or by a broken marriage, or by financial trouble, or sickness, I ask: What is your response to the gospel *now*?

If you truly believed the promise then, you will believe it now. If you did not believe it then but believe it now, well, that is soon enough. Thank God, it is soon enough. But if you are afraid to put your own profession to a test, it is likely that your conversion was not authentic. A genuine conversion to Jesus Christ is undergirded by an autonomous faith which will not discourage a critical self-examination.

When we seek God diligently, it is because we have been persuaded of His integrity to keep His Word. How does God keep His Word? He answers prayer. Our first prayer request to God should have been a plea for mercy on the basis of the shed blood of His Son—a prayer that we might be saved. And God answered. Because of that, we can have confidence that He will answer prayer again and again. The prayer for mercy was the sign of saving faith; from that point on we are in a position to know faith experimentally, even at levels that will exceed our greatest expectations. **"Eye hath not seen, nor ear heard, neither have entered into the heart of man, the things which God hath prepared for them that love Him" (I Cor. 2:9).**

The writer to the Hebrews thus felt a need to pause and make the crucial point found in this sixth verse. If we have understood him—and agreed with him—we qualify for the unspeakable joy of experimental faith. The heroes of faith described in Hebrews 11 had their own theological shock. Yet, they did not draw back; they went on. They believed for themselves—even if nobody else did.

Chapter Seven

Noah: Moving with Fear

Hebrews 11:7

By faith Noah, being warned of God of things not seen as yet, moved with fear, prepared an ark to the saving of his house; by the which he condemned the world, and became heir of the righteousness which is by faith.

One of the interesting things about the way in which these men of faith are referred to is that something slightly new and different concerning the nature of faith itself emerges in each of them. There was therefore no way the writer of the Epistle to the Hebrews could have avoided Noah. For here is a man who bore the stigma of his own generation with such dignity that one cannot but stand in awe of him.

From the account of Noah we learn primarily that if faith is truly to be an enterprise beyond the level of human capability, it will be exercised without the example of an exact precedent or parallel. That which makes faith *faith* is that one is thrust out under the stars, as it were, with no pattern to follow but the promise of God. To put it another way, that which makes the stigma a *stigma* is that it is always new and different. A stigma of its own generation does not remain a stigma; it grows beyond itself to the point that it is eventually hallowed and venerated.

Take Athanasius, for example. Today he is one of the heroes of church history, and to affirm his message—the full deity of Jesus Christ—is hardly to bear a reproach in most Christian circles today. What is a stigma today often becomes a general assumption tomorrow. Those who may have thought that they were bearing the cross of Jesus by praising Christ and not Caesar in the sixth century, for instance, were deluded—that stigma had disappeared centuries before.

Historian Christopher Hill makes the point that one of the tragedies of late seventeenth-century Puritanism was that men were still chewing over what were by then arid doctrines, but which had turned the world upside down the century before. There have always been the Johnny-come-latelies who fancy themselves courageous and righteous because they continue to fight over issues that have been settled long ago.

Noah lived in a day in which there were no architects around who knew about arks. It was a day in which there were no weather forecasters that knew about rain. But God said, **"Make thee an ark of gopher wood"** **(Gen. 6:14),** for **"I will cause it to rain upon the earth forty days and forty nights" (Gen. 7:4).** And what do you suppose Noah's reaction was? He believed God, **"moved with fear"** and prepared an ark **"to the saving of his house."**

Faith's Unique Impediments

Faith, then, is always unique. It is believing God without any prop that one may lean on, whether or not it has been leaned on before. Yes, there is something which all believers have in common; the ground of assurance is always the same for saving faith, and the ground of experimental faith is always the same—believing God. But the uniqueness of faith consists in this: The believer is never allowed to imitate anybody. To the extent that faith is imitated, it is impoverished. "Faith" that is a complete imitation is not true faith at all, but only an enterprise fueled by human ability.

The impediments to faith are never precisely the same in two individuals or in two different eras. Take, for example, two close friends who may have been confronted with the gospel. The impediment to faith for one may be the likely persecution of relatives, but for another it may be the theory of evolution. Each must "go it alone" without destigmatizing the faith to make it something other than faith.

Faith, to be faith, must overcome its own impediment, and the uniqueness of faith consists in the fact that no believer has the luxury of choosing what his impediments will be. What will persuade one person of God's integrity must be independent of what it takes to persuade the next person. When someone says to another, "I'll become a Christian if you will," the subsequent "conversions" of both are very doubtful indeed.

Every person described in Hebrews 11 had in common that he believed God, but never in exactly the same circumstances that had characterized those who had preceded him. The stigma, or impediment to faith, though always equally traumatic, was never presented in exactly the same way. God has a way of boxing us in so that nobody else is involved but Himself. Until we are boxed in that manner, there is no proof that our trust is in His Word alone. It is for our own sake that God does this. Otherwise, we might doubt whether our own faith is authentic. But when one is told to build an ark (when there had never been an ark before), faith has an undoubted opportunity to be unique. Faith is always that way—God sees to it.

Noah was unique in his generation. He was even a man who broke out of his father's mold. Noah had a father who had high expectations of his son. Noah's father's name was Lamech. When Noah came along, Lamech said of him, **"He will comfort us in the labor and painful toil of our hands" (Gen. 5:29 NIV).** Lamech was thinking of his own welfare when he said this, certainly not Noah's welfare. Noah must have grown up under the pressure of knowing that his father had high expectations for him.

Some parents want to relive their own lives through their children in order to compensate for their own failures. If they can see their children do what they couldn't, it hopefully relieves them of some guilt, or lets them live twice, as it were. Noah's father wanted his son to make life easier for him. But building an ark probably wasn't exactly what his father had in mind.

In this connection it is very interesting that both Luther and Calvin had fathers who had high expectations for their sons. Luther's father wanted young Martin to be a lawyer so that he could care for his father in his old age. Both Luther and Calvin eventually broke out of their fathers' molds and lived under their fathers' disapproval. This is what happened to Noah.

Noah was unique also in that he stood out in bold contrast to the general atmosphere of his day. Noah lived in a time of violence, unrestrained sexual activity and pleasure. **"God saw that the wickedness of man was great in the earth, and that every imagination of the thoughts of his heart was only evil continually"** (Gen. 6:5; see also Gen. 6:4, 11).

Jesus said that in Noah's day there was **"eating and drinking, marrying and giving in marriage"** (Matt. 24:38). Faith enables one to be different in any age, but when one lives in such a day as Noah's, there is a clear opportunity to stand tall. Morality alone would practically make one unique, but to have genuine faith in a day like Noah's is to be unique indeed.

The chief thing about his uniqueness is this: **"Noah found grace in the eyes of the Lord"** (Gen. 6: 8). What a contrast in Genesis 6! **"But Noah"**! It is one thing to break out of your father's mold, still another to be moral and transparent in a wicked and evil age. **"But Noah found *grace* in the eyes of the Lord."** This statement explains what was at the bottom of Noah's uniqueness. He did what he did because of God's grace and that is always the only hope that anybody has. While Genesis 6:8 tells us that Noah's secret was grace, Hebrews 11:7 says it was faith. Is this a contradiction? Never. **"For by grace are ye saved through faith,"** said Paul (Eph. 2:8). Grace is the underlying cause; faith is the precipitating cause. And that is always the order.

And yet the uniqueness of Noah on which the writer to the Hebrews seizes is that Noah was warned of God **"of things not seen as yet"** (Hebrews 11:7). All that we have observed above with regard to Noah's uniqueness was only God's preparation for the chief work for which he was raised up. God has a way of sharpening our perception, personality and even lifestyle along the way that gives a hint of His ultimate work for us. Clyde Narramore has said that our gifts are often God's hint as to what we should do with our lives.

Noah was being dealt with along the way, but there came a time when his call to uniqueness transcended all else that was true: He was warned of things **"not seen as yet."** This calling not only separated him from his parents and his own generation, but from history as well. He had no historical precedent to which he could point that would convince his contemporaries that he was on the right track. There was no tradition that was built around the idea of **"rain to come."** Neither could Noah go into a yacht showroom and select the most suitable ark for his family.

When one stands for something **"not seen as yet,"** he always looks like a fool, or, at best, the embodiment of arrogance. Whether at the level of nature (as in a new discovery or invention) or of faith (as in a theological innovation), the person who holds forth an idea **"not seen as yet"** is looked upon with great suspicion. And why not? People are not unjustified in looking upon the innovator with suspicion. Therefore the man who is motivated by things **"not seen as yet"** should be particularly patient and understanding towards those who cannot see what he sees. Were it not for the natural suspicions of others, there would be no stigma or impediment to faith at all. Their suspicions make faith possible!

What, then, convinces another that a man such as Noah could be right? Answer: that he moves with godly fear. Noah **"moved with fear"** (*eulabetheis,* **"moved in godly fear"**). When a person is running scared because he has seen a vision of the Most Holy God, it becomes obvious that this person isn't trying to be clever or different. He is authentically motivated and such genuineness is manifest. All the preparations that preceded Noah's vision at this stage of his life were insignificant by comparison. But this vision was it. Noah knew it. God spoke and Noah was never the same again.

What was so moving about Noah's preparing of the ark, then, was Noah himself. People may have laughed and scoffed at the ark. But they didn't laugh at Noah. When a man is moving with holy reverence and godly awe, it is no laughing matter. However innovative Noah's ark was, the faith he demonstrated was not something to be taken lightly.

One cannot but compare Noah's motivation with most theological ideas of this century. This has been the century of theological innovation (although much of it is nineteenth-century liberalism in new dress). This is the century of "crisis theology," "process theology," "theology of hope," and "God is dead." The one thing that stands out is cleverness; the one thing that is missing is godly fear.

I have yet to read the first line of the theological innovators of the twentieth century that made me feel they were moving with godly fear. I've been greatly impressed with brilliance, originality, erudition and prose; but never have I been driven to my knees in prayer and worship, or with the desire to have more of the anointing of God on me, by reading contemporary theology. Theologians used to be men of God; now they are men of ideas. Today's theologians may point us to things **"not seen as yet"** and they might even build their arks—but not with godly fear, as Noah did. The missing note in theology today is the fear of God.

The Legacy of Faith

Noah's moving with fear did not save millions or even thousands, but it did save his own family. I regard this as a remarkable accomplishment. When faith leads anyone to the **"saving of his house,"** it is very valuable indeed. From one point of view, this is what gave Noah's faith its greatest uniqueness of all. His was a day of marrying over and over again—families weren't staying together. But Noah saved his family. When a man saves his own household, it tells you a lot about that man. It tells you that those who were closest to him believed in him the most.

Winning thousands is one thing, but it is quite another to win the respect of one's wife and children. If you ask what is the surest way to win your children—I answer—a father moving with godly fear. Over the years people have come to me and asked what is the secret of my knowing the Bible. Actually, my love for the Word of God began at an early age. I knew what it was to see my father on his knees in worship for half an hour every morning before he went to work, and his example instilled in me a hunger to know his God.

Someone once said of me that I came to Trevecca College (where I first trained for the ministry) with more knowledge of the Bible than most students left it with. That is not a compliment to me but to my father. My mother said of my father that he was the best Christian she knew.

How did Noah save his family? First, Noah saved them by example: **"Noah was a just man and perfect in his generations, and Noah walked with God" (Gen. 6: 9).** Second, they were saved by teaching them. He was called **"a preacher of righteousness" (II Pet. 2:5).** He warned all men of the approaching flood but succeeded only with his children. Nevertheless, I regard that as successful preaching indeed.

Whereas Noah did not save the world, he nonetheless left the world without excuse. Our writer tells us that the uniqueness of Noah consisted also in this, that **"he condemned the world."** His moving with fear, his building the ark and his saving his family left the world without any excuse. This, ultimately, is our only responsibility. We may not save all—not even our families—but we can leave them without excuse. This is what is meant by condemning the world. He condemned the world by his marked contrast to it—that made the difference.

If Noah had been like everybody else, he could never have left them without excuse. The problem with the modern church—and too many parents in it—is that we are so like the world that there is no contrast by which to condemn it. We live in a godless age, but it gives us an easy opportunity to be unique. As Theodore Beza once said, "The color black is never better set forth than when white is set by it."

The last thing our writer says about Noah pertains to the benefit he received as a consequence of his faithfulness. Noah became **"heir of the righteousness which is by faith."** The doctrine of justification by faith did not begin with Luther or the Apostle Paul, nor even with Abraham or Noah. For it had been true since Abel's day. Those living in Old Testament times were saved just like those in New Testament times—by faith. All that Noah did was by faith. This faith did quite a lot, not the least of which was this: Noah himself was saved.

Chapter Eight

Abraham: Not Knowing Whither

Hebrews 11:8

By faith Abraham, when he was called to go out into a place which he should after receive for an inheritance, obeyed; and he went out, not knowing whither he went.

Abraham, the first great patriarch of the Old Testament, who was to Israel second only to Moses in stature, occupies nearly one-third of the eleventh chapter of the Epistle to the Hebrews. Abraham is mentioned in the New Testament no fewer than seventy-four times. He was Paul's example for justification by faith (that is, how we are justified before God) and James' example of justification by works (that is, how we are sanctified before God). He is the only person in the Bible who is called God's **"friend" (Isa. 41:8; James 2:23).**

The Jews regarded Abraham as their biological father (John 8:33), but Paul argued that what matters ultimately is whether Abraham is our father at the level of the Spirit—by faith (Gal. 3:9, 29). The writer to the Hebrews will bring this point home in a succeeding study regarding Hebrews 11:19, perhaps the most profound verse to be dealt with in this book.

The writer to the Hebrews mentions Abraham several times in his epistle. Referring to Jesus, he says that Christ took **"not on him the nature of angels; but he took on him the seed of Abraham" (Heb. 2:16).**

Abraham's example prefigured the New Testament doctrine of assurance: **"For when God made promise to Abraham, because he could swear by no greater, he sware by himself, saying, Surely blessing I will bless thee, and multiplying I will multiply thee. And so, after he had patiently endured, he obtained the promise" (Heb. 6:13- 15).** The seventh chapter of the Epistle to the Hebrews mentions Abraham several times in connection with Melchisedec. Thus, Abraham's emergence in Hebrews 11 is something of a continuation; and, although his name only appears twice in this chapter, at least twelve verses are centered on him.

Between the time of Noah and that of Abraham, there was one major event in the world that will bear mentioning: the confusion of tongues that resulted from the building of the Tower of Babel. Until the building of this tower, the whole earth was of one language, though we do not know what language it was. But the wickedness of man was manifested in this proposition: **"Let us build us a city and a tower, whose top may reach unto heaven; and let us make us a name, lest we be scattered abroad upon the face of the whole earth" (Gen. 11:4).** God was displeased with this, so He came down from heaven and confounded their language. There were ten generations between Shem (the son of Noah) and Abraham, and apparently there was no one among them whom the writer to the Hebrews could single out as an example of faith.

There is no indication that the true worship of God was carried on throughout these ten generations. If anything, they began to deny God's honor entirely, for we read in Joshua 24:2, **"Your fathers dwelt on the other side of the flood in old times, even Terah, the father of Abraham, and the father of Nachor: and they served other gods."** Rather than being a godly man, Terah, Abraham's father worshiped **"other gods."**

Abraham therefore was not brought up in a godly home. He was not catechized or exposed to any sound confession of faith. He was probably a sun-worshiper. That was Abraham's heritage. Noah broke out of his father's mold; but Abraham did this in a much more remarkable way, for he had no godly heritage at all. Neither was there any hint of a godly atmosphere around Abraham prior to the time that God revealed Himself to him.

Calling Precedes Preparation

We may refer to God's revealing Himself to Abraham as Abraham's "calling." Our verse says, **"By faith Abraham, when he was *called*..."** All greatness may be traced to one's calling, and so with Abraham. The calling took place in this fashion, when the Lord first spoke to **"Abram"** (as he was known at first): **"Get thee out of thy country, and from thy kindred, and from thy father's house, unto a land that I will show thee" (Gen. 12:1).** But there was this further word to him, and it came as a *promise:* **"And I will make of thee a great nation, and I will bless thee, and make thy name great; and thou shalt be a blessing" (Gen. 12:2).**

One interesting thing about the call to Abraham was the promise of greatness. And yet the very thing that made God angry with regard to the Tower of Babel was that people were going to make a name for themselves. But here we find God saying to Abraham, **"I'm going to make you a great name."** Is there a contradiction?

God is not against greatness—as long as He is the architect of it. He resists the proud, but gives grace to the humble (I Pet. 5:5). But if we are thinking of making ourselves great and building a name for ourselves, we will be fighting against God. One of the most common temptations for a Christian, especially if he is involved in Christian service, is to think he must build up a certain image—or build up his name, as one would do in show business. The parallel between show business people and some Christians in the Lord's work is one of the most ominous signs of twentieth-century Christianity.

Jesus said, **"Ye are they which justify yourselves before men; but God knoweth your hearts: for that which is highly esteemed among men is abomination in the sight of God" (Luke 16:15).** It is a melancholy commentary on contemporary Christianity that some preachers and evangelists, singers and musicians that go out in the name of the Lord often give the impression they are far more interested in their names and their careers and their reputations than they are in the glory of the Lord. If anything is sadder than that, it is this verse: **"And he gave them their request; but sent leanness into their soul" (Psalm 106:15).** My predecessor,

Dr. Martyn Lloyd-Jones, once said to me, "The worst thing that can happen to a man is for him to be successful before he is ready."

God promised to make Abraham a great name, but not before Abraham was ready. Indeed, Abraham had much to go through before he was ready. God delights in making men great—provided that He is the One doing it. God may be calling you who read these lines to greatness. You may think you are the most insignificant person on earth. But God's calling sometimes begins in a remote corner of the earth. It can begin in a lowly place, in unlikely surroundings, in an "impossible" situation. It can begin when all men doubt you, when all misunderstand you.

This is precisely the way it was with Abraham. One might even call it the essence of his call, for he gave no hint of promise—either by background, reputation, qualifications or strategic location. He had absolutely nothing going for him. But God delights in selecting people like that! He who created all things "out of nothing" continues to make men great who hold no promise whatever. **"The last shall be first" (Matt. 19:30).**

How did Abraham know that his calling was real? How did he know that it was God talking? How did Abraham know that he was not deceived? Have not men been deceived before, thinking they had a call from God when they didn't? Was Abraham taking a chance? Was this venture an "existential leap" (as some put it today)? Consider these words: **"Get thee out of thy country and thy kindred, . . . into a land that I shall show thee" (Gen. 12:1).** How did Abraham know that his call was real? He knew because the call of God is always self-authenticating. It leaves a man knowing in his heart of hearts that God has spoken.

The call of God authenticates itself by virtue of the One who gives the call. Only God can call someone and leave him dazzled and staggered with the realization that it could never have been his own projection. A natural religion is, as Feuerbach put it, man's projection upon the backdrop of the universe.

Abraham was a sun-worshiper, and he certainly wasn't expecting God to talk to him. Men may read astrology charts (it is reported that fifty million Americans take their own astrology charts quite seriously), but the predictions of astrology never succeeds in producing the inner persuasion that they are truly authentic—especially when the charts vary among themselves. That which separates *God* from the *gods* of natural religion and superstition is that He is the *living* God—He is alive! King Darius said to Daniel, **"I make a decree, That in every dominion of my kingdom men tremble and fear before the God of Daniel: for he is the living God"** **(Dan. 6:26).** Peter said to Jesus, **"Thou art the Christ, the Son of the living God" (Matt. 16:16).** Abraham knew that he was being confronted by the living God.

Not only that, the living God always takes the initiative. With natural religion, or existentialism, or humanism, you must *do* something—start it, get it going, initiate it, put it to work. But the living God is the one who *calls*. He beckons and makes us aware that we had nothing to do with it.

Take the case of Nathanael. His immediate reaction to Jesus of Nazareth was: **"Can there any good thing come out of Nazareth?" (John 1:46).** Shortly, however, Nathanael was found asking Jesus, **"Whence knowest thou me?" Jesus answered, "Before that Philip called thee, when thou wast under the fig tree, I saw thee" (John 1: 48).** The image of God in man leaves man restless and searching. As St. Augustine put it, "Thou hast made us for Thyself; our hearts are restless until they find their rest in Thee."

Natural religion leaves man thirsty, but the true God leaves a man with conviction and persuasion. When we have heard from the living God, we are aware in our deepest being that we could not have merely projected it. Abraham knew he was not deceived. As John Calvin once put it, "When first even the least drop of faith is instilled in our minds, we begin to contemplate God's face, peaceful and calm and gracious towards us. We see Him afar off, but so clearly as to know we are not at all deceived." The primary attribute of faith is that it is grounded upon God's promise.

Affirmation Comes Before Confirmation

The nature of the promise of God to Abraham was unconditional. God did not say, "If you will do this, then I will do that." Rather, God said to Abraham, "You *will* do this and I *will* do that!" *"Get thee out of thy* **country, and from thy kindred, and from thy father's house, unto a land** that I will show thee: And I will make of thee a great nation, and I will bless thee..." (Gen. 12:1-2). It was not a conditional proposition; it was simultaneously a command and a promise. Why? Because God does not affirm us on the basis of what we do—He affirms us because of what *He* does. "I will have mercy on whom I will have mercy," He says (Rom. 9:15). He does not affirm us upon conditions, He affirms us *as we are*.

Just as I am without one plea,

But that Thy blood was shed for me,

And that Thou bidst me come to Thee,

O Lamb of God, I come.

Affirmation comes before confirmation. God affirms us before He confirms us. The way He did it with Abraham was that He *told* him before He *tried* him. God always passes us before He tests us. He persuades us before He perfects us and assures us before He authenticates us. This is the way God works: He approves us before He proves us. By this we know the whole time that we are accepted.

God's call to Abraham was effectual. "By faith Abraham, when he was called...obeyed." The proof of God's call to Abraham was that it secured the desired response. Grace always comes in this manner. God does not say, "I will choose you if you believe." Rather it is this: "I have chosen you, you therefore believe." Said Jesus, "Ye have not chosen me, but I have chosen you." (John 15:16). As John put it, "We love Him, because He first loved us" (I John 4:19). Saul of Tarsus learned this on the road to Damascus. Ananias confirmed what Saul already knew in his heart of hearts: "The God of our fathers hath chosen thee, that thou shouldest know his will, and see that Just One, and shouldest hear the voice of his mouth" (Acts 22:14).

I do not say that men do not reject the gospel. Of course they do, for it is happening all the time. But the case of Abraham is the only explanation why some *do* accept the gospel! For if God did not go to special pains with some, none would ever be saved. Abraham's calling was self-authenticating and effectual. "For many be called, but few chosen" (Matt. 20:16). The call of Abraham corresponds to what our Lord meant by "chosen" in the aforementioned verse.

Abraham's call, however, meant separation. Abraham was called **"to go out into a place which he should after receive for an inheritance"** **(Heb. 11:8). "Get thee out of thy country and from thy kindred" (Genesis 12:1).** God's call always demands separation. In fact, the very *nature* of the call assumes a separation. The word "church" comes from the Greek *ekklesia*, which means **"the called out ones."** Life in Abraham's day had degenerated to an exceedingly low ebb: generation after generation gave no indication of trust in God. Then came the Tower of Babel. Abraham's father had turned to **"other gods."** Abraham's call was, **"Get thee out of this place."**

Abraham's Stigma

Every generation has its stigma by which the believer's faith is tested. What was Abraham's stigma? It comprised three things. First, he had to leave *home*. Not that he minded that, for nothing is ever quite the same after faith sets in. Faith instills the impossible. Temporal things are replaced by things eternal. The same things to which we were so attached take on a different meaning. Second, Abraham had to leave his *family* as well. **"Get thee out of thy country and from thy kindred."** But even this was not as difficult as one might suspect, for once faith sets in, old friends—even family—never look the same again. The strongest bond on the earth is Christian fellowship.

But the third thing about Abraham's stigma was what made things truly difficult: He had no proof to offer another person that he was right. **"And he went out, not knowing whither he went."** He obeyed because he knew. But he couldn't convince another person that he knew. That is often the essence of the frustration we face as believers. The natural wish is for personal vindication—"If only others could see what I see and feel what I feel! Why won't God show them?"

Abraham's stigma was that **"he was called to go out into a place which he should after receive for an inheritance."** Had he been given the inheritance before he went out, there would have been no stigma at all, neither would there have been any faith. But the reproach for Abraham was that he proceeded upon the basis of Divine guidance alone, heading toward a strange country, content with the honor of God alone. We may indeed want to vindicate ourselves, but we all learn—sooner or later, **"Vengeance belongeth unto me, I will recompense, saith the Lord"** (**Heb. 10:30).** You may want that other person—perhaps even a close relative—to see that you are right. But you must let God handle that part. The essence of a stigma is to be content with the honor of God while everybody calls you a fool.

What about Abraham's confirmation? Did God confirm Abraham? The answer is, yes—but not immediately. It is required of faith to be content primarily with God's affirmation of us, and to proceed upon the basis of His affirmation before we are confirmed by outward signs. That is naked faith. You go out, but you don't know where you are going. God passes us before He tests us. Faith is accepting His verdict that we have passed—that we have been justified already. Then we pass the test by accepting God's verdict. We accept the stigma before we have the confirmation, but the whole time we know that we are not deceived—God passes us. That is enough.

Chapter Nine

Abraham: In a Strange Country

Hebrews 11:9

By faith he sojourned in the land of promise, as in a strange country, dwelling in tabernacles with Isaac and Jacob, the heirs with him of the same promise.

Few men in history have been tried as severely as Abraham. God promised Abraham that he would become the father of a new nation and that Abraham would have a great name. But there is little evidence that Abraham himself enjoyed such prestige. Abraham's life was nomadic in nature. He lived in tents. He remained a stranger the whole time he lived in the land of promise, for his eyes were focused on things beyond his natural life.

What made Abraham great? Clearly it was the *trial* of his faith. Not merely his faith by itself but the trial of it. Peter said it is **"the trial of your faith"** which is **"more precious than of gold that perisheth" (I Peter 1:7).** Abraham was a man of great suffering. This is, in fact, what made him great. It also explains the absence of greatness on the horizon at the present time. There is a dearth of truly great men today, both in the church and in government. Men want the short cut to greatness; we want to bypass suffering.

Part of Abraham's suffering consisted in the nomadic nature of his life. After leaving home, he stopped in Haran and eventually made it to Canaan—the **"land of promise."** In other words, once Abraham crossed over the border into Canaan, he had arrived in the land to which he was called. This was it. "We're here," Abraham might have said to himself. "You're there," God might have whispered. By faith he obeyed the call to the land which he would "after" receive for an inheritance. "This is it." Here it was—Canaan.

But there was no welcoming committee sponsored by the Canaanites, with signs waving, "WELCOME, ABRAHAM, TO THE LAND OF PROM-ISE." There were no bands playing, or choirs singing, "Is not this the land of Beulah?" The Mayor wasn't there to give Abraham the key to the city. Abraham might have asked, "Is that all there is?" All that was present was the same voice with which Abraham had become familiar, the voice that said, "Get thee out." The voice now said, "This is it." But there were no choirs, no bands, no fanfare, no welcoming committee—no external con-firmation. Only God's voice. But that voice was enough. It meant so much to Abraham that he built an altar at a place near Bethel in order to thank the Lord.

Yet wasn't this a rather lackluster beginning for Abraham in the land of promise? It was no small matter for him to leave his homeland. Surely, having reached his goal, should there not be some outward confirmation that he had done the right thing? All Abraham had was the witness of the Spirit at this stage. He may have looked across the fields and the hills and valleys of Canaan and wondered what God saw in this land.

What made Canaan the land of promise was not what could be seen with the natural eyes, but what was affirmed by God's Spirit. What made the land of promise the land of promise was precisely the *absence* of bands playing and flags waving. Had the welcoming committee been present with the Mayor presenting the key to the city, it could not have been called the **"land of promise"**—for no faith would have been required.

It was **"*by faith* he sojourned in the land of promise, as in a strange country."** The designation **"land of promise"** was given by the writer to the Hebrews to show what makes faith *faith*. We should be thankful for this. Indeed, thank God for the land of promise. What is your land of promise?

It may be elsewhere, or it may be where you are right now. Perhaps you want to be relocated? If God keeps you where you are, it may well be that the very absence of what appears promising is God's opportunity to show His power. The grass is always greener on the other side of the fence.

All of us know the joy of fantasy in anticipation of a coming event. It may be looking forward to a holiday, but often the preparation for it is more exciting than the holiday itself. And yet, that is often our own fault. We should not live in a dream world. Take marriage, for example. Many marriages are on the rocks partly because the dream and the reality were so different from each other.

The same is true of a new job or any kind of new setting. Disappointment often stems largely from unrealistic expectations. It may well be that your land of promise is where you are right now. After all, leaving your present residence, or job, or dissolving your marriage only means starting again somewhere else. With men things are impossible, but with God all things are possible (Matt. 19:26).

Internal and External Confirmation

Our verse shows two types of confirmation: the *internal* confirmation and the *external* confirmation. The internal confirmation is essentially the same thing as God's affirmation (sanctioning) of us. It is the internal testimony of the Holy Spirit (as Calvin called it). It is sufficiently powerful that one is held steady in the face of conflicting winds. The essence of faith is this inner witness of the Spirit. This is really all that Abraham was going on at this stage. **"By faith he sojourned in the land of promise."**

What is the external confirmation? It is the tangible outworking of things when things "fall into place." For example, it may be a wonderful answer to prayer—the sort of thing that can be of tremendous encouragement. It may be the providence of God in your affairs so that things take place in such a manner beyond your own manipulation that you know only God could have done this or that. Such is an external confirmation. It is tangible, something you can see. Sometimes the external confirmation is no more than a word of approval from an authority figure. It might even be your self-conscious willingness to do God's will and to heed His voice.

There are, however, certain principles with which we ought to be familiar in connection with these two kinds of confirmation. The first principle is this: The internal witness should always be the primary confirmation. Otherwise you will derive your primary witness at a human or materialistic level. The weakness of our flesh yearns for the external confirmation (which requires less faith). God does us a singular favor when He postpones the external confirmation. For in the postponement of outward signs you have a wonderful opportunity to grow. It is the time you discover whether you will be tested and will trust God's word alone.

The second principle is that the external witness (or confirmation) is often but a merciful concession of God to the weakness of our flesh. The writer to the Hebrews, having stressed that the nature of faith is to believe the promise alone, made this concession to these weak Christians who ought to have been much further along (Heb. 5:12): **"God is not unrighteous to forget your work and labour of love" (Heb. 6:10).** He repeated this encouragement in Hebrews 10:32-35. But it was mostly a concession to them.

Yet all of us need God's external confirmations. He knows how much we can bear (I Cor. 10:13). **"He knoweth our frame; He remembereth that we are dust" (Psa. 103:14).** He gives external confirmations not a moment later than we can endure without them, and not a moment sooner. God is never too late and never too early, but always just on time.

There is only one person who ever lived who never needed an external confirmation: our Lord Jesus Christ. For His faith was a perfect faith, and He was given the Spirit without measure (John 3:34). Just before Jesus raised Lazarus from the dead, He prayed, **"I knew that thou hearest me always: but because of the people which stand by I said it, that they may believe that thou hast sent me" (John 11:42).** Perfect faith requires no external confirmation.

The more faith we have, the less we need external confirmation. But because of the weakness of our flesh, God will sometimes grant external confirmations to bolster the faith we already have. Abraham's faith was of such a high degree that he mostly seemed content with having only the *internal* confirmation which came from communing with God.

The confirmation that came again and again to Abraham was simply God's voice. *The* voice. God would say to Abraham, "Look at the stars. Count them. Look at the sand. Count the grains. So shall your seed be." But the confirmation was really no more than what God said the first time (Gen. 15:5; 12:1). This shows that the internal confirmation may be strengthened by a simple reminder of God's promises already received.

The third principle with regard to the two kinds of confirmation, then, is this: the longer we can postpone the external confirmation, the more significant it will be when it comes. If we have to be served with continual external confirmations, then the great things God may do for us later won't mean as much as they should when they come. God wants to reserve the peak experiences for us, so we might enjoy the full inner satisfaction for having waited!

When the writer to the Hebrews said, **"by faith Abraham sojourned in the land of promise, as in a strange country,"** he described primarily a faith that was nourished by an internal confirmation. Abraham was nourished by God's voice—the promise. The word.

But our verse goes on to say that Abraham dwelt in tabernacles **"with Isaac and Jacob, the heirs with him of the same promise."** This positively shows that Abraham was eventually given great external confirmations. What was the great external confirmation of Abraham's life? The birth of Isaac. The original promise was: **"I will make *of thee* a great nation" (Gen. 12:2).** But Abraham waited a long time before there was an Isaac. The writer of the Epistle to the Hebrews therefore also describes the external confirmation to Abraham's faith; he was given a son—and a grandson! Not only that, his offspring kept the faith. We are told that they were **"heirs with him of the same promise."** Nothing is more gratifying for a parent than to have his children embrace the promise of God.

A Stranger in a Strange Land

There is another thing in this verse that must be considered: Abraham never forgot that he was in a **"strange country."** Although he had set foot in the **"land of promise"** it was always a strange land to him. Abraham always considered himself an alien, a foreigner in Canaan. Abraham never "settled in." He was always a stranger, not because of where he came from but because of where he was going. Yet, he had all of the benefits of the land and became Canaan's most famous citizen!

The irony, if not the secret, of life itself is this: When we see the transitory nature of life, we make the greatest contribution to the world. When we are most detached from the world, we make the greatest contribution to it. We are not ready to live until we are ready to die. Better still, we cannot live until we do die. Through regeneration (being born again) our **"old man"** died, and so we are admonished to reckon ourselves as **"dead" (Col. 3:3; Rom. 6:11).**

Though Abraham was detached from the land, look at his contribution. He became the father of all the faithful. And it is interesting that, although he never settled in, he had all the benefits of the land. It is when we abandon our right to ourselves that we find ourselves. **"For whosoever will save his life shall lose it, and whosoever will lose his life for my sake shall find it" (Matt. 16:25).**

Abraham was detached from the land but had all he wanted from it. He lived in tabernacles—tents—because he was convinced of the transitory nature of life. But when we are the least attached to earthly things, we enjoy earthly things most. When we are too attached to something, we are in greatest danger of losing it. When we follow the internal witness of the Spirit through God's word, He has a way of eventually showering us with external benefits that go beyond anything we dare ask or think!

However, Abraham had a severe trial in this **"land of promise."** Soon after he arrived in Canaan the land was besieged with famine. If ever there was an absence of the external confirmation, surely this was it. Where are the grapes of Eshcol in this land of promise? Where is the milk and honey? He finds instead a famine in the land. At that point anybody could have easily said to him, "You are a fool."

But this is why we should never depend too much upon the external confirmation. Why? Because the absence of the external witness is not necessarily a sign we are not in God's will. Abraham no sooner arrived in the land which he was to receive as an **"inheritance"** than he found it was anything but a lovely garden. **"And there was a famine in the land: and**

Abram went down into Egypt to sojourn there; for the famine was grievous in the land" (Gen. 12:10).

Yet the famine in Canaan is not the worst thing that happened to Abraham once he began following the Lord. It is at this stage that we see one of the saddest episodes of Abraham's life. Let us tiptoe up to the window and look in. We do so quietly, but thank God we can look in. For it is helpful that this event was recorded.

One wonderful thing about the Bible is that it does not cover up the blemishes of the great saints. So here it tells what happened, in hopes that you might be encouraged to know that Abraham, the great man of faith, fell prey to unbelief. He did. It lets us see that a man of faith sometimes experiences doubts. Here was Abraham in the land of promise with famine in the land. What was he going to do? He would go down to Egypt.

Once Abraham made the decision to go to Egypt, he began projecting. His projection became the vehicle of his unbelief. What is a projection? It is a defense mechanism by which we superimpose our own fears onto our ideas of another's actions. The extreme form of it is paranoia. Projection is possibly the most dangerous of defense mechanisms, especially if we do not realize that is what we are doing.

Abraham projected that Pharaoh would find his wife attractive. He was right in that projection. He also projected that the only way he could live in Egypt was to tell a lie about his wife and say that she was his sister. But in this he was wrong, and this is where his projection led him to unbelief. For Abraham had already been promised that he would be a father of a nation, and yet in this situation he seems to have concluded that he would surely die before ever becoming the father of a nation.

Abraham thought he had to keep himself alive by telling a lie. This was indeed a melancholy moment in his life. Look at him. What a pitiful man this man of faith has become. Abraham was now watching his own wife being escorted into Pharaoh's palace. How do you think Abraham felt? What would his friends have said now? Abraham must have thought to himself, "How did I ever get myself into a mess like this? Could this really be happening to me?" Here was Abraham in a compromising, humiliating situation. He was a long way from home, a long way from Ur, and a long way from God's calling. There he was, without the remotest external confirmation that he was a real man of God. He could only trust God.

All Abraham could do now was to watch God work. We are told that God sent plagues on Pharaoh's house, and when Pharaoh found out that Sarah was Abraham's wife, both of them were let go—which further shows that Abraham's projection was wrong (Gen. 12:17-20). Abraham left Egypt and headed straight for Bethel (Gen. 13:3), the place where he had once demonstrated his gratitude to God—a good place for a backslider!

The writer to the Hebrews does not tell us about Abraham's sojourn in Egypt. For this episode is hardly an example of faith or faithfulness. What we do know is that Abraham was delivered from this folly. His sin did not abort God's purpose or plan for him. For we know that Isaac and Jacob eventually came along—**"the heirs with him of the same promise."** It was a demonstration of the truth of Romans 8:28 long before Paul articulated it.

God has a way of sanctifying to us our deepest distress, even by shaping our past! Canaan was a strange country, but Egypt was stranger still. Egypt, however, made Canaan look like the happiest place on earth. Wherever Abraham would go in this world he would be a stranger in any case, but he learned it is better to be a stranger in the land of promise than a compromiser anywhere else. It is better to be in the will of God without the external confirmation, even in famine, than to be out of the will of God with all its inevitable sorrow.

Chapter Ten

Abraham: Looking For a City

Hebrews 11:9-10

By faith he sojourned in the land of promise, as in a strange country, dwelling in tabernacles with Isaac and Jacob, the heirs with him of the same promise: for he looked for a city which hath foundations, whose builder and maker is God.

It is our task in this chapter to capture the essence of Abraham's greatness, his real genius. Abraham was a great man, one of the greatest men in the history of the human race. True greatness is an exceedingly rare quality. A man may be famous, or admired, or even loved, and not be great. He may have marvelous gifts and not be a great man. Abraham was a great man. What made him great? In other words, what was his genius? The Jews undoubtedly regarded Abraham as a truly great man, but did they know what his genius was? I think not.

We find an illustration of this in the history of Calvinism. One of the most pertinent observations ever made about Calvin was that his followers by and large missed his real genius. They were so close to him and so uncritical of him that they could not see what made him what he was; consequently, they were not able to interpret him accurately. So with Abraham and the Jews. **"We are Abraham's seed,"** they would shout defiantly, but the great pity was that they understood Abraham least of all.

The writer to the Hebrews understood Abraham. It is therefore not surprising that Abraham gets more attention in the eleventh chapter of Hebrews than any other Old Testament figure. You will perhaps say that the genius of Abraham was his faith. You would be right, but there is not a Jew who ever lived who would disagree with this. Everybody knows about Abraham's faith. One must go deeper than that to discover Abraham's genius.

As with anyone, genius and motivation are closely akin. To uncover anyone's genius, you must find out what motivates them. Is it ambition? Is it self-esteem? Is it a desire for power? Is it to be remembered in history? Is it knowledge? Is it wealth? Is it sex? Is it family? Is it fear? We could go on and on with this line of questioning, but none of these will bring us any closer to understanding this man Abraham.

What then was the essence of his greatness? Was it his sojourns in Egypt? Obviously not, for this was one of the darkest episodes of his life. Was it in his leaving his own country and walking out under the stars, **"not knowing whither he went"**? Well, perhaps, but that doesn't tell us much about his motivation. Was it living in the land of promise **"as in a strange country"**? Yes, but this only points to what he did, not to what caused it.

You may think Abraham's greatness was related to his detachment from material things, like money. Indeed, Abraham was a wealthy man, and yet he never gives the impression that money meant much to him. When he encountered a petty problem with his nephew Lot, Abraham simply said, **"Look at the land. You pick what you want, and I'll take the rest" (Gen. 13:9).** That illustrates what greatness is. But it does not tell what lies behind it. Consider also the episode of the slaughter of kings in Genesis chapter 14. Abraham returned the spoil lest the king of Sodom should claim he had made Abraham rich (Gen. 14:23). Here is greatness.

But why could Abraham do this? Why was he detached from material things? Why was he able to leave home and live all his life in a strange country? What lay behind his great faith? The answer to these questions, and the only explanation for what followed with regard to Abraham's extraordinary faithfulness, lies in this short verse: **"For he looked for a city which hath foundations, whose builder and maker is God."** In a nutshell, Abraham was on his way to heaven, and knew it. So claims the writer to the Hebrews.

As the Jews have misunderstood their hero Abraham, so have many Christians missed the genius of Christianity. What is the genius of Christianity? It is this: We are going to heaven, and we know it. If we lose this motivation, we cease to be authentic Christians and we make Christianity into something it was never meant to be.

What often happens with us is that we confuse cause and effect. As the great English martyr John Bradford aptly put it when describing his encounter with certain "free-willers" in the King's Bench prison, "The effects of salvation they so mingle with the cause." For example, consider the fact that a by-product of Christianity seems always to be the raising of living standards when it penetrates a pagan land—intellectually, culturally and economically. What motivated the original missionaries? It was not, I promise you, to raise living standards! It was to make men fit for heaven. But there were certain "effects" that seemed to follow.

The folly of missionaries of succeeding generations has been to go to foreign soil to reproduce the *effects* that came about when early missionaries preached. The rise of living standards is but an accidental effect of the gospel. Nothing is more self-defeating for the Christian faith than to primarily seek the achievement of certain effects among men. The genius of Christianity is the message of heaven and hell. I can recall as a boy being thrilled over stories of returning missionaries concerning glorious conversions. But today? Returning missionaries are more likely to talk of glorious hospitals, highways, agricultural improvements, overcoming cultural barriers, new techniques in medicine and dentistry, and so forth. Mere effects.

The burden of the writer of the Epistle to the Hebrews was to show the heavenly nature of faith. He wants us to know that faith ultimately derives its source and motivation from this: We are going to heaven, and know it. Take this away from Christianity and you have severed the jugular vein. According to Paul, **"if in this life only we have hope in Christ, we are of all men most miserable" (I Cor. 15:19).** That is a far cry from the popular saying that if there were no heaven to gain or Hell to shun, it would still be worth being a Christian. "Nonsense!" cries Paul, and so also says our writer to the Hebrews. The one thing that kept Abraham going was this: **"he**

looked for a city which hath foundations, whose builder and maker is God" (Hebrews 11:10).

Dwelling in Tents

Abraham dwelt in tabernacles—**"tents."** The Greek word is *skenais*, the word used in John 1:14; **"The Word was made flesh and dwelt (tabernacled, *eskenosen*) among us."** We have a parallel: both Jesus, who had *perfect* faith, and Abraham, who had *great* faith, **"tented"** among us. **"Foxes have holes, and birds of the air have nests; but the Son of man hath not where to lay his head" (Luke 9:58).** As noted earlier, Abraham was a rich man. He surely could have purchased real estate from the Canaanites. It would have been easy for him to buy hundreds of acres and make that **"land of promise"** the ultimate realization of everything, the final *eschaton*! But he didn't. For had he done it, it would have ceased to be the land of promise.

Abraham was looking for a city, and he knew that when God made the promise, He did not have merely an acre or two in mind. It was something far more vast than that. What a pity when people sell themselves short of the ultimate thing God has in mind and settle instead for just a little bit in the here and now. This is why Jesus warned: **"If thy hand offend thee, cut it off: it is better for thee to enter into life maimed, than having two hands to go into hell, into the fire that never shall be quenched" (Mark 9:43).**

You might say, "For Abraham to dwell in tents wasn't all that bad if he had all that money." Perhaps. Abraham's wealth was indeed some measure of compensation on this pilgrimage. God knows our need, and He will put upon us no more than we can bear. There is no trial allowed but what is **"common to man" (I Cor. 10:13).** Moreover, not only did Abraham need his wealth as a compensatory factor in the lifestyle God called him to, but Genesis 14 says he actually needed every penny of it when he was involved in the slaughter of the kings and the rescue of Lot!

Abraham was given wealth basically for two reasons: He needed it and he could be trusted with it. Most of us do not need it; neither can we be trusted with it. Most of us have all we can handle. God does us a special favor by keeping us from great riches. Though we may tend to cast an envious eye on those who have more than we do, consider this: If they are real Christians, we should assume that they need it and also that they can be trusted with it.

Rather than coveting the wealth of others, we would do well to be sure that God can trust us with what He has already given us. In any case, Abraham's wealth was incidental to him. The norm of his life was dwelling in tents, and his primary motivation was looking for a city in heaven rather than one on earth.

Not only did Abraham live in tents, but we are told that he passed this lifestyle on to his son and grandson. He dwelt **"in tabernacles with Isaac and Jacob."** All of us as parents know the feeling of wishing we could do more for our children than we are able to do. Do you ever say to yourself, "What a pity that I must pass this way of life on to my children"? Abraham passed on to his children a lifestyle of dwelling in tents. Abraham may have wished that his sons could have seen the countryside of Ur and been reared in the kind of atmosphere he himself was brought up in.

As a child I would fantasize about having a different set of parents. I would sometimes say to my father, "I wish I had what so-and-so has." My father would look me in the eye and say, "Son, your dad works for wages. I'm sorry. We can't afford that." Sometimes my own son will say to me, "Why can't I do what so-and-so does?" I answer: "Son, you are being brought up in a Christian home. There are some things we don't do. Someday you will have your own family, and then you can live as you please. But as long as you are under this roof, you will go to church, hear the Bible read in the home, and there will be certain things you will not do."

Abraham dwelt in tents. He passed that lifestyle on to Isaac. And what do you suppose Isaac did with it? He continued it. He, too, dwelt in tents. Isaac passed this way of life on to Jacob. And Jacob dwelt in tents. Abraham passed on to his son the greatest inheritance a father could ever give a son—the promise of God. Perhaps we as parents wish we could do more for our children. But remember, if we pass on to our children the promise of eternal life, we give them the greatest inheritance of all. We are told that

Abraham dwelt in tents, but so did Isaac and Jacob—**"the heirs with him of the same promise."** The promise!

Compare Abraham, Isaac and Jacob. Each of them was different. Abraham was undoubtedly the greatest of the lot in stature. Isaac was probably the most lackluster figure in the whole of the Old Testament. About all we know about Isaac is the promise God gave to Abraham regarding him and the way in which Rebecca manipulated Isaac so that the poor man didn't even get his way in giving blessings to Esau. The three men were markedly different: Abraham, Isaac, and Jacob. Yet they were **"heirs of the *same* promise."**

One of the great things about the promise is that we are not required to be what we are not. We don't have to pretend. Some of us have lesser gifts and abilities, but we are heirs of the same promise. Do you realize that Christianity is the only religion in the world that lets men truly become what they are? What is the gospel? It is the promise of God that there is a heaven. A Christian is one who lives by the promise, not by what he thinks he must do or be to please another person. Christianity does not seek primarily to produce a certain effect, whether in terms of a kind of personality, or brand of piety, or particular mannerism. The same promise allows each of us to become what we are. What are we? The way God made us.

It is the gospel alone that maximizes God's creation of us and the creative possibilities within us. There is the expression, "When God made so-and-so He threw the mold away." It is only through the gospel that we know God *always* throws the mold away! We are to be ourselves; neither must we reproduce a certain effect that may have been authentic in another person or another generation.

Abraham's greatest problem, however, was not his lifestyle or any concern he may have had about passing on to Isaac a lifestyle of living in tents. His concern was whether there would ever *be* an Isaac! For in the various internal confirmations God would give to Abraham there was this word **"seed."** God said to him, **"I will make thy seed as the dust of the earth: so that if a man can number the dust of the earth, then shall thy seed also be numbered" (Gen. 13:16).** Again, "Look now toward heaven, and tell the stars...So shall thy seed be" (Gen. 15:5).

This word "seed" must have caught Abraham's ear. Abraham had no son at all, and his wife Sarah was barren. Perhaps Abraham was tempted to think, "Surely this was an unguarded comment by the Lord." "Seed?" We often find things in Scripture we don't understand. Some things look as if there were an error here or there, or perhaps an idle or unguarded comment. It is the internal witness of the Spirit that drives us on, for God will in time make every single word plain. Those who will not wait for God's explanation rush at their peril toward a premature explanation—that which is commensurate with the natural and rationalistic level. "Seed?"

THE CITY FROM HEAVEN

What kept Abraham going? He was looking for a city. What enabled him to be so magnanimous with Lot? He was looking for a city. What kept him motivated even though he did not understand all he perceived to be of the Lord? He was looking for a city. The best way to keep out of trouble is to look for a city whose builder and maker is God. It is the best way to overcome the petty problems that would divert us from what really matters. Christianity becomes what it was never meant to be when the vision of that city gets explained away. Christianity only turns the world upside down when it has that city in view.

Abraham was actually **"looking"** for a city. The Greek is *exedecheto*, which is in the imperfect tense: "was looking." The word actually means **"to wait for"** or **"to expect."** When did he look for that city? All the time! Faith sees things other people do not see. Faith elevates one into the realm beyond the level of human understanding or capability. It is something which non-Christians cannot understand. For there is a motivation that is so forceful and strong that it transcends all earthly activities. And what is that? Looking beyond the natural realm. We wait for it. Why? Because we are persuaded that God's promise is true.

Where did Abraham expect to find that city? Not in Canaan. For if he had looked for it in Canaan, he could have started his own city. He had the money; he had the family. He even had 318 slaves. He might have said, "I have the promise of a city. This is it." But Abraham had a different kind of city in mind—a city that had foundations (unlike tents), whose builder and maker is God. Abraham knew that he would not be the architect of such a monumental undertaking, for this was far beyond the level of his competence. He recognized that only God could construct the glorious city he saw afar off.

There's a land that is fairer than day,

And by faith we can see it afar;

For the Father waits over the way

To prepare us a dwelling place there. —S. F. Bennett

John the Apostle was given a closer look at the city. **"I John saw the holy city, new Jerusalem, coming down from God out of heaven, prepared as a bride adorned for her husband" (Rev. 21:2).** Then John said he heard a great voice: **"Behold, the tabernacle of God is with men."** Tabernacle of God? Tent of God? Does God dwell in a tent? Even *God's* dwelling place is now temporary, for until the Final Day, God's dwelling place is called a tabernacle. One day, though, He will dwell with men in an eternal city, where **"they shall be His people, and God Himself shall be with them, and be their God" (Rev. 21:3).**

At that stage John said a voice summoned him, **"Come hither, I will show thee the bride, the Lamb's wife. And he carried me away in the spirit to a great and high mountain, and showed me that great city, the holy Jerusalem, descending out of heaven from God" (Rev. 21:10).** John was given a close look at that city whose builder and maker is God. It had walls and gates and **"twelve foundations" (Rev. 21:14).** Not only that, **"the city had no need of the sun, neither of the moon, to shine in it: for the glory of God did lighten it, and the Lamb is the light thereof" (Rev. 21:23).**

What a city! Abraham seems to have seen it first. He saw it afar off, but one glimpse kept him going. Tents did not matter. Wealth did not matter. Petty problems did not matter. What mattered? That city. Abraham knew it would be worth waiting for. He knew it was the best inheritance to pass on to Isaac. He convinced Isaac and Isaac convinced Jacob; for they were all heirs of the **"same promise."**

What a city! Abraham certainly could not have created it, for any city he would create would have wicked men dwelling in it. But he waited for a city which excluded **"the fearful, and unbelieving, and the abominable,**

and murderers, and whoremongers, and sorcerers, and idolaters, and all liars" (Rev. 21: 8). Any city which Abraham would have created would have included tears, death, sorrow, crying and pain. Instead, he was looking for a city in which God would **"wipe away all tears from their eyes,"** where there would be **"no more death, neither sorrow, nor crying, neither shall there be any more pain: for the former things are passed away" (Rev. 21:4).**

What a city! Seeing the vision of it was Abraham's genius.

Chapter Eleven

Abraham and Sarah

Hebrews 11:11

Through faith also Sarah herself received strength to conceive seed, and was delivered of a child when she was past age, because she judged him faithful who had promised.

The vision which Abraham had of the Heavenly City not only kept him going, it enabled him to accomplish much on this earth. We are not ready to live until we are ready to die. Abraham by now has already had a remarkable career and has accomplished enough to earn the title **"man of faith (Gal. 3:9)."** But in fact he has only begun, for the things which we tend most to know about Abraham are events which the writer to the Hebrews has not yet dealt with. All that Abraham has experienced up to now is but God's preparation for *the* work Abraham must yet do.

It is remarkable that God should take the time to prepare us for our ultimate work. Such preparation is usually in the context of what we think is surely that ultimate work already. And yet we need always to think that what we are doing at the moment is the main work God has in mind for us, or we would likely not take the present task too seriously.

By now Abraham might well have been a tired man who could look back upon his life and say to himself, "I've had a good life." He has, in John Newton's words, been through "many dangers, toils and snares." But the fact is that Abraham's chief work lay in the future. All up to now was but preparation.

At this stage in our study of the people of faith, Abraham is called upon by the writer to step aside, as it were, and share some of the glory with Sarah his wife. The **"men of faith"** that we think of in Hebrews 11 actually include two women by name—Sarah and Rahab the harlot (verse 31)—but also revolve around two other outstanding women, Moses' mother (verse 23) and Deborah, the main figure in the life of Barak (verse 32). The writer thus dignifies women generally and the possibilities of faith in women particularly.

Sarah's Faith

The writer tells us that through faith **"also Sarah herself"** *(kai aute Sarra)* indeed accomplished something extraordinary. The Greek usage stresses that it was Sarah's *own* faith; *kai*, which in this case should be translated either **"also"** or **"even,"** combined with *aute* the reflexive pronoun, indicates that the writer wants us to see that Sarah's own faith lay behind what follows. Yet she could not have accomplished what she did apart from Abraham. The two of them together eventually came to believe that God would give them a son. But the writer indicates that it was Sarah's faith that resulted in their having a son, **"because she judged him faithful who had promised."**

On the other hand, if we read through the original account in Genesis we are rather hard-pressed to see much indication of Sarah's faith. One might easily believe the opposite, that Sarah had no faith at all! We shall consider this apparent contradiction. Why did the writer think that Sarah **"herself"** had faith? Whereas in Genesis there is little hint that Sarah believed, in Hebrews 11 there is little hint that she doubted. Can both accounts be true?

We begin with the obvious fact that Sarah was barren. The writer's word is *steira*—**"barren,"** or **"past age"** (KJV). This in itself may have brought certain psychological pain to her, for it is natural for most women to want to have a baby. But that was not the real problem. The real problem was that Abraham had been given a promise long before which assumed he would eventually be a father.

The original promise from God to him was, **"I will make of thee a great nation" (Gen. 12:2).** This was enlarged upon afterwards, specifying that the one who **"shall come forth out of thine own bowels shall be thine heir" (Gen. 15:4). "Look now towards heaven, and tell the stars, if thou be able to number them: and he said unto him, So shall thy seed be" (Gen. 15:5).**

It was precisely this promise to Abraham that became the ground of his justification by faith (see Gen. 15:6). It was this word that the Apostle Paul seized upon in Romans 4:3. No doubt Abraham eagerly shared the promise with Sarah. How do you suppose that made Sarah feel? She was barren and growing older every day. Great emotional pressure was on her to prove God's promise.

Both Abraham and Sarah began to think they had misunderstood God's promise, or perhaps miscalculated it. Abraham began to think that his offspring must come through his servant Eliezer (see Gen. 15:2). After all, Eliezer was a member of the family (as servants were in those days), and his heir could surely count as Abraham's (so thought Abraham). To dispel such reasoning, God told Abraham the heir would come forth **"out of thine own bowels" (Gen. 15:4).**

But Sarah had an idea too. Her solution to the problem was to nudge the arm of God's providence and make Hagar, her servant and handmaid, the channel of blessing (see Gen. 16:2). After all, Abraham would thus be the real father, and the promise would fit perfectly which said, **"out of thine own bowels."** Since Hagar was a member of the family, surely there would be no problem. In one way of looking at it, such a solution was most magnanimous on Sarah's part. But she was under such pressure to produce a child that the matter of letting her husband sleep with Hagar became the happiest solution she could think of. She wanted the whole thing to be over and done with.

Is this then what the writer to the Hebrews meant by Sarah's faith? Surely not. Manipulating prophecy and providence may partly demonstrate that one believes God's infallible Word, but it fully demonstrates sheer unbelief in God's ability to *keep* His promises! Sarah's faith was not demonstrated in her solution pertaining to Hagar, but rather in a most interesting story recorded in Genesis 18. Three visitors, probably angels (see Heb. 13:2), unexpectedly paid Abraham a visit. Abraham accepted them and asked Sarah to provide a special meal for them.

Laughing at God

While preparing the meal, Sarah overheard what to her was a most incredible conversation. One of the angels made a prediction to Abraham that within *one year* (a point the King James Version does not make clear) **"Sarah thy wife shall have a son" (Gen. 18:10).** When Sarah heard that, she **"laughed within herself" (Gen. 18:12).** But almost simultaneously with Sarah's laughing to herself, she heard the angel quite abruptly ask Abraham, **"Wherefore did Sarah laugh?" (Gen. 18:13)** and then told Abraham virtually what had gone on in Sarah's mind.

Sarah's faith was born in that moment. Her laughter was suddenly turned into godly fear. The overheard conversation had become the word of the Lord to her own soul. Sarah was confronted with the matter of her laughing. At first she denied laughing. Why? Why should Sarah deny laughing? Was not her laughing a most natural, if not honest, response to that extraordinary conversation?

The answer is that Sarah immediately realized that she was laughing at God. That Sarah should be confronted with a matter which the angel could not have known about unless he spoke for the Most High God sobered her sooner than she could bat an eyelash. How could the angel have known that Sarah laughed to herself? There could be only one answer— God alone was behind the entire conversation which she overheard.

It was no laughing matter at all. **"Then Sarah denied, saying, I laughed not; for she was afraid. And he said, Nay; but thou didst laugh"** (Gen. 18:15). Sarah was sobered but also assured when she heard these words as well: **"Is any thing too hard for the Lord?" (Gen. 18:14).** For the first time, Sarah could see for herself that the living God was indeed at work. She was not laughing now—she believed. From that moment on **"she judged him faithful who had promised."**

The writer to the Hebrews got it right. Sarah was afraid because she believed. Her fear was her faith. She saw that God was dealing with her as He had been dealing with Abraham. Until that moment she thought that any communication with God was strictly between her husband and God. But now she knew that she was included, too. They were in a ministry together! She was never the same again.

There is a great lesson for us here, with particular reference to the marital relationship. It applies not only to the ministry but also to any Christian marriage. The wife needs to know that God deals with her too! No wife can fully support her husband until she believes that God wants her involved. She must feel that not only does her husband want her support, but God does as well.

Nothing is more encouraging to a Christian wife than the obvious dealings of God directly with her. She needs to see the unmistakable hand of God for herself. A wife can take her husband's word of assurance only for so long. Sooner or later she must see God's intervention for herself, or she will drag her feet and drain the marital relationship of strength. Nothing is more defeating for the husband than an unbelieving wife. (The reverse, that of the unbelieving husband, is also true of course.)

It is a most wonderful thing when the wife is given a witness of God's dealings in such a manner that there is no natural explanation for such an occurrence. It may be that she will need to have the fear of God put upon her. But when God deals with the wife in as definite a way as He does with the husband, it is a sure sign of God's seal upon that marriage and of wonderful things to come. Abraham had believed; now Sarah believed. She too **"judged Him faithful who had promised."**

The writer of the Epistle to the Hebrews tells us how God brought His promise to fulfillment. The account in Genesis simply states that the time came when the Lord visited Sarah, and she conceived (see Gen. 21:1). The writer to the Hebrews said that Sarah herself **"received strength to conceive" (Hebrews 11:11).** Here was a woman who was ninety years of age; she was indeed quite beyond the **"manner of women" (Gen. 18:11).**

There was no way, physically speaking, that she could have a child. But by this time she believed that nothing was too hard for the Lord. She may have walked the floor in the meantime, wondering how this would in fact happen. The answer is: She **"received strength to conceive."**

It was an accomplishment beyond herself. It was out of her hands. God has a way of bringing us to the place where we must leave everything utterly to Him. Sometimes He refuses to use us until we do exactly this—leave things entirely in His hands. He brings us to humiliation and near despair so that we will see that things have been taken out of our hands in order for Him to do things His way. God does this so that later on we will not be able to take any credit for His work and think a particular accomplishment was something we did.

GRACE FOR THE MOMENT

You may ask, "How will I cope with this?" I answer: You will be given strength. Your strength will come no sooner, no later, than when you actually need it. But such strength will be there in time and will come in such a manner that defies explanation at a human level.

Corrie ten Boom tells of asking her father, "What is it like to die?" He answered her, "When we take the train to Amsterdam, when do I give you the ticket to hand to the guard?" She replied, "Just before we get off." Her father then added, "That is the way God deals with us." God answers our questions when we really need the answers. God supplies the grace when we really need it. **"As thy days, so shall thy strength be" (Deut. 33:25). "Take therefore no thought for the morrow: for the morrow shall take thought for the things of itself. Sufficient unto the day is the evil thereof" (Matt. 6:34).**

God gives the ticket when we need it—no sooner. **"Is anything too hard for the Lord (Genesis 18:4)?"** Whether we are facing a major decision; sorrow or bereavement; misunderstanding or perhaps depression over having been accused of poor judgment, illness, or anxiety over the results of an examination—God's grace is never wasted by being given to us before we need it.

Why did God allow Abraham and Sarah to reach the ages of one hundred and ninety respectively before giving Sarah such **"strength to conceive"**? Could not God have let Isaac come when Sarah was in her twenties or thirties? All of us have questions like this. Why does God let this happen to me? Why didn't God do this sooner? Why didn't God stop that? Or why did God permit Abraham to lie with Hagar? Have you ever considered the sorrow that the world has known as a result of Abraham and Hagar?

There are no sure answers to questions like these. To look for answers is an exercise in unprofitable speculation. We must leave these matters to the hidden wisdom of God. What matters is whether we know this:

All the way my Saviour leads me;

What have I to ask beside?

Can I doubt His tender mercy

Who thro' life has been my guide?

Heav'nly peace, divinest comfort,

Here by faith in Him to dwell!

For I know, whate'er befall me,

 Jesus doeth all things well.   —F.J. Crosby

As for Abraham and Hagar, the result was Ishmael. Sarah's solution became everyone's sorrow. It was a mistake that Abraham and Sarah had to live with for the rest of their lives. Grace does not erase history. Grace does not efface the past. Ishmael was now on their hands, if only for them to learn that Ishmael was not what God had in mind.

Sarah's folly, however, did not remove her from God's purpose for her. **"He hath not dealt with us after our sins; nor rewarded us according to our iniquities" (Psalm 103:10).** For God not only had Abraham in mind, but also Sarah rather than Hagar. Sarah's natural explanation of God's promise to her husband could not have been more wrong, but it did not make God change His mind either! Even Sarah's laughing at God did not make Him change His mind. For God was determined to deal with Sarah herself and make her see His glory.

Sarah's natural explanation for God's promise and her natural reaction to His own purpose for her have been repeated by all of us many times. We are all like Sarah. We have manipulated providence and prophecy and judged His promises incredible. But God has also been kind to us as He was to Sarah—even turning our laughter to godly fear. It is a sign that He is dealing with us, that He wants to include us in His great purpose. His dealing with us is treating us with dignity even though we have not so treated Him.

The modern church is like Sarah. Barren. Past age. But let us not laugh at what God would do in our generation. The trend can be reversed—overnight. One year from now we might look back on what we thought was impossible. "He who laughs last laughs best," said Shakespeare. God rebuked Sarah for laughing, but let her have the last laugh. For she said when Isaac came along, **"God hath made me to laugh, so that all that hear will laugh with me"** (Gen. 21:6).

Once they laughed at her, but now they laughed with her. So men may laugh at us for a time, but God can make them laugh with us. Sarah had the last laugh. So will we. The gates of hell shall not prevail against the church.

His purposes will ripen fast,

Unfolding every hour;

The bud may have a bitter taste,

But sweet will be the flower.

—William Cowper

Chapter Twelve

THE SEED
OF ISAAC

Hebrews 11:12-16

Therefore sprang there even of one, and him as good as dead, so many as the stars of the sky in multitude, and as the sand which is by the sea shore innumerable. These all died in faith, not having received the promises, but having seen them afar off, and were persuaded of them, and embraced them, and confessed that they were strangers and pilgrims on the earth. For they that say such things declare plainly that they seek a country. And truly, if they had been mindful of that country from whence they came out, they might have had opportunity to have returned. But now they desire a better country, that is, an heavenly: wherefore God is not ashamed to be called their God: for he hath prepared for them a city.

Since the chapter we are studying deals largely with certain Old Testament personalities, there may be a temptation for us to move on to Hebrews 11:17 at which point our writer returns to the expression "by faith." But to do that would suggest that we are missing the very point he wanted to make when he brought in these illustrious names in the first place. It would be a great pity to read this famous "faith chapter" of the Bible but miss the writer's thesis. He is far more interested in telling us something about faith itself than he is in describing what these great men did (which those Hebrew Christians already knew about anyway).

The writer's thesis is that faith is essentially spiritual and supernatural in character; that is, it is an enterprise beyond the natural level. The writer believes this so strongly that he breaks the pattern he has followed up to now and develops quite a new theme. The new theme is *the basis of continuity of Abraham's seed from one generation to another.* I must admit that we are now embarking upon one of the most difficult concepts to grasp but one that is very rewarding indeed if we will follow the writer of our epistle very carefully. I suspect this point of view has been largely overlooked by many who have written commentaries on Hebrews 11.

Part of the problem is the way Hebrews 11:12 is interpreted—**"Therefore sprang there even of one, and him as good as dead."** If we understand what our writer meant by these words, we will have less trouble grasping the most difficult verse in our chapter—Hebrews 11:19—regarding the meaning of receiving Isaac **"in a figure."** Hebrews 11:19 is the conclusion of this new section, and we do ourselves no favor if we rush on to verse 17 merely to get back to his expression, **"by faith."** Indeed, the writer of our epistle doesn't really get back to his previous manner of writing until he comes to verse 20.

Why, then, should the writer of our epistle take eight verses between the birth of Isaac and the elderly Isaac blessing Jacob? These eight verses tell us virtually nothing about Isaac! (There isn't really much he could have told us about Isaac in any case, for Isaac is the most colorless of the patriarchs—if not also of all whose names are mentioned in Hebrews 11.) There is only one answer, and that is that the writer of our epistle sees something significant regarding the nature of faith that demands an apparent digression in order to bring out the meaning.

Who Was the One "as Good as Dead"?

The first question is: Who is the **"one"** in verse 12? **"Therefore sprang there *even of one*."** The answer: Isaac. It is often thought that the writer was referring to Abraham and that the writer's expression **"him as good as dead"** refers to Abraham's age—one hundred. Yet, Isaac was the one meant in verse 11, without any doubt; he was Abraham's natural **"seed"** and the child who was born to Abraham and Sarah. It was from Isaac, then, that there sprang **"so many as the stars of the sky in multitude."**

Could not the same be said of Abraham? Yes, but that would be to miss the writer's point.

However, didn't God make a promise to Abraham when He said to him, **"Look now towards heaven, and tell the stars...So shall thy seed be" (Gen. 15:5)?** And does not Hebrews 11:12 go back to this same promise when the writer refers to **"so many as the stars of the sky in multitude"?**

Although the answer is "yes" to both questions, to leave it at that could still be to miss the point. For example, take this promise: **"I will multiply thy seed exceedingly, that it shall not be numbered for multitude" (Gen. 16:10).** Or another: **"Behold, I have blessed him, and will make him fruitful, and will multiply him exceedingly; twelve princes shall he beget, and I will make him a great nation" (Gen. 17:20).** And also this: **"Arise, lift up the lad, and hold him in thine hand; for I will make him a great nation" (Gen. 21:18).**

These three promises in the Book of Genesis don't refer to Isaac at all, but rather Ishmael. These promises sound an awful lot like the one originally given to Abraham, and also like what our writer is talking about in Hebrews 11:12. So if our writer meant Abraham as the **"one,"** we would have to include Ishmael and his succeeding generations as equally a part of the **"stars of the sky in multitude,"** for Ishmael indeed was a son of Abraham. And whereas those proud Jews retorted to Jesus, **"We be Abraham's seed" (John 8:33),** let it never be forgotten that any Arab up to the present day can equally truthfully say the same thing!

That is precisely why our writer could never have meant Abraham as the **"one"** in Hebrews 11:12. For if Abraham were the **"one,"** then there would be no need for faith; the continuity of Abraham's seed from one generation to another would be based upon nature—procreation alone. Any Jew and any Arab could equally lay claim to being children of Abraham. There would be no need whatever for faith; one would only need to be born in a Jewish or Arabic household.

It was that very mentality that Jesus was up against (and Paul as well) when He spoke of the true nature of Abraham's seed. For a Hebrew Christian the hardest thing of all to give up was his natural heritage. Paul, however, gave it up with such joy that he regarded the **"flesh"** as **"dung"** **(Philippians 3:3-11),** but most needed a little time to absorb that hard concept, not to mention rejoice in it. These Hebrew Christians were being instructed anew in the true basis of the continuity of Abraham's seed.

This **"one,"** then, was not Abraham himself but Isaac, but was not Isaac Abraham's natural son? Was it not Abraham's own seed that was impregnated in Sarah's womb? Did not Isaac come along by procreation? Yes, but Abraham was shortly to learn a lesson, the hardest lesson that any of us has to learn, namely, that we are not our own. Abraham was ordered by the Lord to offer his son Isaac as a burnt offering. Abraham agreed. Abraham went all the way in carrying out God's orders, and when Abraham lifted the knife up in the air to bring it down upon Isaac's body, there was no thought that this mission would be aborted. For Isaac was **"as good as dead."**

Isaac was as good as dead as far as Abraham was concerned; he was as good as dead as far as he himself was concerned. But at the very last moment—in a split second—God intervened, aborted the mission and said to Abraham, **"Now I know that thou fearest God, seeing thou hast not withheld thy son, thine only son from me" (Gen. 22:12).** And from Isaac alone, although utterly given up by his father, there sprang **"so many as the stars of the sky in multitude, and as the sand which is by the sea shore innumerable" (Heb. 11:12).**

It might be countered by some that Paul used a similar expression in Romans 4:19, and obviously Abraham was meant: **"And being not weak in faith, he considered not his own body now dead, when he was about an hundred years old, neither yet the deadness of Sarah's womb."** My reply is that the writer of the Epistle to the Hebrews (even if it was Paul) wanted to show not only the miraculous nature of Isaac's own birth (that Sarah was "past age") but equally the supernatural character of Isaac's subsequent seed. Hence the words, *kai tauta nenekromenou*—**"even this one was dead" (Heb. 11:12).**

The words **"as good as dead"** are probably a fair interpretation of the Greek, but it literally means that this one was actually dead, *nenekromenou* being a perfect passive participle. Whereas in Romans 4:19 it is said that Abraham **"considered"** or **"faced the fact"** that his own **"body"** *(soma)* was dead, the writer to the Hebrews is not speaking of how Abraham regarded his body, but how the death of Isaac would have made any offspring impossible forever. Our writer will elaborate on this in verse 19. At this stage he simply wants to show that from **"one"** there sprang **"so many as the stars of the sky."**

But why the stress on **"one"** (Greek *enos*, **"of one"**)? Because the number that is analogous to the sand by the sea did not spring from two—Isaac and Ishmael—but one, Isaac only. If it is Abraham's seed to which the writer is referring, then one must let Ishmael in on everything. The supernatural character of Abraham's seed is completely lost if the offspring must include the sons of Ishmael. But no! There sprang **"even of one, and him as good as dead, so many as the stars of the sky."**

If there is any remaining doubt about this, it is put away by the following verse 13: **"These all died in faith."** How could the writer make a claim like that? How could he be so sure that a number **"as the sand which is by the sea shore"** died in faith? Is he sure that all of these had faith? He clearly says that **"these all"** *(pantes)* died in faith. Was this an unguarded comment? It was not. The writer meant exactly what he said, and this is the reason why the **"one"** must be Isaac rather than Abraham. Those who sprang from one **"as good as dead"** are none other than heirs by faith!

All heirs by faith have this in common: they, too, were as good as dead but have been quickened (Eph. 2:1). The reason our writer can be so sure that this innumerable company died in faith is that there was a *particular kind* of seed that would typify the sons of Abraham via Isaac: They were not sons by procreation but by regeneration.

The True Sons of Faith

It follows, then, that not only are all of Abraham's natural children not to be reckoned his true sons, neither are all of Isaac's seed. For if procreation were to be the basis of continuity of Abraham's seed from one generation to another, then every Jew and every Arab would be declared children of Abraham. It follows that if procreation were to be the basis of the continuity of Abraham's seed, then so also must every natural heir of Isaac be reckoned as children of Abraham—both Jacob and Esau, the twelve tribes of Israel, etc. This is precisely why Paul said, **"For they are not all Israel, which are of Israel" (Rom. 9: 6).** What makes us heirs of Abraham is *faith*—whether we be Jew or Gentile!

At this point our writer gives more details regarding the nature of faith; indeed, how all the innumerable spiritual heirs of Abraham came to believe. What follows is an *ordo salutis* **(order of salvation)** that is valid for any age; indeed, the only order that is ever valid. Although these heirs did not receive **"the things promised"** (NIV), they had in common this order: (1) they were persuaded; (2) they embraced; and (3) they confessed.

We have already had occasion to look at this matter of the *ordo salutis* (see Chapter Two). The *ordo salutis* is one of the best places to begin if anyone wishes to refine his theological perception. To be able "to think theologically" is a neglected element among Christians today, but one which is able to increase your faith; indeed, to by-pass "thinking theologically" is to miss a blessing that will not be known by any other route.

The way Old Testament saints came to believe is no different from that which is presented in the New Testament. They were persuaded; they embraced; they confessed. The persuasion was in the *heart;* the embracing was in the *will;* the confession was with the *mouth.* Nothing has changed. **"For with the heart man believeth unto righteousness; and with the mouth confession is made unto salvation" (Rom. 10:10).** It must be said that there has been a tendency in modern Christianity to reverse this order. Many are made to confess Christ before they have truly embraced Him; much less have they been persuaded.

One of the effects of existentialism is the emphasis upon the will without reference to what the mind first conceives as valid. This is a day of irrational thinking. It is a day of doing rather than thinking. That which gives rise to so many false professions of faith, whether in churches or evangelistic campaigns, is that people confess before they embrace, and even embrace before they are persuaded.

It is often a feeling of guilt and anxiety that motivates people to by-pass a correct order of salvation. They are so anxious to do what they perceive is a good thing that they do not take the time to think the matter through. Churches are filled with non-thinking Christians partly for this reason. Whether they can properly be called Christians is open to serious question.

The writer of the Epistle to the Hebrews shows us how the seed of Isaac came to believe. A person is first persuaded by seeing *(idontes)*, then he embraces or welcomes *(aspasamenoi)* what he sees afar off. The proof, then, that he has indeed welcomed the promise is that he confesses *(homologesantes)*. And what is the nature of this confession? They confessed that **"they were strangers and pilgrims on the earth."** The nature of every credible profession of faith is that the convert now knows this world is not his home. He is going to heaven and knows it.

That is what makes a profession of faith a true one. He is not only persuaded of this, then, but he embraces it with his whole will. What is more, he is not ashamed of it. He confesses it. As King David put it, **"For we are strangers before thee, and sojourners, as were all our fathers: our days on the earth are as a shadow"** (I Chron. 29:15).

Extraterrestrial Vision

At this stage our writer reverts to the point he had made about Abraham, namely, that faith always has an extraterrestrial vision and motivation. Faith sees the transitory nature of this life and this world. The reason why the writer brings in this theme again is that there were those who would object to all he has said on the basis that the notion of heaven is a New Testament innovation. He has already shown that faith itself is not a New Testament innovation, but now his task is to show that the very idea of seeking a city beyond this life is equally nothing new. This is why he says, **"For they that say such things *declare plainly* that they *seek* a country"** **(Heb. 11:14).** Our writer believes that he has dealt with that objection once for all.

There is yet another objection which he anticipates: that some would say these Old Testament saints considered themselves strangers simply because their origin was ultimately different from the country which they happened to be inhabiting. In other words, one may counter our writer by saying, "Look. Abraham was a stranger because he was from Mesopotamia." The same sort of objection could be applied to many of these saints— that they happened to be living in a country different from that in which they were born. According to this objection, it was their origin, not their destination, that made them think as aliens.

"No!" thunders our writer. **"If they had been thinking of the country they had left, they would have had opportunity to return" (Heb. 11:15 NIV).** What made them strangers, then, was their destination, not their origin! If it was their origin that made them strangers, why didn't they go home? Answer: Home to them was what they were looking forward to, not where they came from. Just as faith is not a New Testament innovation, neither is heaven. That, in a word, is our writer's conviction concerning the kind of faith that they had.

A wonderful consequence follows for those who have true faith, a two-fold result in fact: God's approval now and heaven to look forward to in the future. **"God is not ashamed to be called their God: for he hath prepared for them a city" (Heb. 11:16).** There is to be seen in the ones who have true faith something to be cherished above anything else in this world: the knowledge that God is not ashamed to be called our God. God proved that He was not ashamed to be called their God when He revealed Himself to Moses at the burning bush: **"I am the God of thy father, the God of Abraham, the God of Isaac, and the God of Jacob" (Exod. 3: 6).**

The highest compliment and the most singular honor ever bestowed upon a man is that God is not ashamed to be his God. For when God declares Himself in this manner, He puts His name and honor on the line. What a marvelous thing that God should let His own name be associated with the names of mortal men when He wants to distinguish Himself from idols!

Why was God not ashamed to be called their God? Answer: because they were not ashamed of Him. These men did not take their cue from nature; they saw what others in their generation did not see. They saw beyond nature, that God had something better prepared for them. And they confessed to the same.

Jesus said, **"Whosoever therefore shall be ashamed of me and of my words in this adulterous and sinful generation; of him also shall the Son of man be ashamed, when he cometh in the glory of his Father with the** holy angels" **(Mark 8:38).** If you are ashamed of God, He will be ashamed of you. Jesus also said, **"Whosoever therefore shall confess me before men, him will I confess also before my Father which is in heaven" (Matt. 10:32).** God is not ashamed of us when we are not ashamed of Him.

The knowledge in the here and now that God is not ashamed of us may be called *heaven on earth.* For the knowledge that God approves of us and affirms us right now is a little bit of heaven to go to heaven in. And yet this little bit of heaven is not heaven. To put it another way, some people think the only hell is the portion of hell they are experiencing on earth. But that is wrong; hell on earth is not hell. There is a hell that comes at the end of every sinful life. And so with heaven; God has prepared **"a city."**

The ultimate proof of His approval of us is the fact that He has prepared for us **"a city."** God looks forward to showing it to us. Jesus has been preparing that place for over nineteen hundred years. **"I go to prepare a place for you" (John 14:2).**

For whom? The seed of Isaac. And such are we. By faith.

Chapter Thirteen

Abraham and Isaac

Hebrews 11:17-18

By faith Abraham, when he was tried, offered up Isaac; and he that had received the promises offered up his only begotten son, of whom it was said, That in Isaac shall thy seed be called.

The account of Abraham's offering up Isaac is one of the best known but also most controversial stories in the Bible. The story embodies what modern theology calls "mythology" in Scripture. This event, possibly more than any other, gives rise to what some theologians refer to as the cruelty of the God of the Bible. It is this very event that has "emancipated" some from a need to be faithful to Scripture, for this account to them is the ultimate proof that the true God and the God of Scripture are not necessarily one and the same.

I have a theory regarding the story of Abraham and Isaac. I suggest that the account (which I believe was literally true) demonstrates the difference between being a **"son of haste"** and a **"son of promise."** My frame of reference for these nicknames is the account of Sarah and Hagar. When the promise which God made to Abraham was not soon fulfilled, Abraham was baffled. He could not understand why God should talk about his **"seed"** being as the stars in the sky when Sarah year after year was not even pregnant.

One day Sarah came up with an idea—**"Sleep with Hagar my maid,"**—she suggested (Gen. 16:2). After all, Hagar was like a member of the family; her child would still be Abraham's seed (which would keep the promise intact), so surely this is what God must have had in mind all along. Abraham agreed, and he slept with Hagar—as a result, Ishmael was born. "The promise has been fulfilled at last," Abraham may have thought. But Abraham was wrong. God said of Sarah, **"I will bless her, and give thee a son also of her" (Gen. 17:16).**

Abraham laughed at this, but it turned out that Ishmael was not the promised child after all. He came along because Abraham and Sarah could not wait for God to keep His promise by Himself. They nudged the arm of Providence. Ishmael—the son of haste—was the unhappy result. A **"child of haste"** is always the unpleasant consequence of following one's natural instinct as opposed to following the Spirit (even though it may take some time before one realizes that a mistake has been made after all). Those who rush to a natural conclusion with regard to biblical infallibility do so because they are following their natural instincts rather than the Spirit.

No story in the Bible illustrates the stigma of faith so dramatically and faithfully as this one does. Every generation has its stigma by which the believer's faith is tested. Faith is always believing without the evidence. No mortal man was tried as Abraham was. His trial was quite severe before Isaac finally came along. But he eventually failed that test, and he had to live with his mistake. The sorrow that followed as a result of Hagar's Ishmael (see Gen. 16:4 and 21:9-14) is an undoubted illustration of how all of us must live with our past sins—even if they have been forgiven.

We cannot change the past. Or erase it. And yet, it is thrilling to know that God still let Abraham have another opportunity to pass the test of experimental faith. We are not talking about saving faith. Abraham's saving faith was noted in Genesis 15:6, and the righteousness that was put to his credit would never be withdrawn.

But God gives to the man of faith an opportunity also to be justified by works, as James put it (Jas. 2:21-26). Justification by works is passing the test of experimental faith. It is when we ourselves actually do something (albeit by faith) which pleases God. Many of us fail at this, especially the first time. Abraham did. But God came to him a second time. Jonah did. But God came to Jonah the **"second time" (Jonah 3:1).** He does this to all of us, for He's the God of the "second look," as John Newton put it.

Abraham's Test

The original account of God's testing Abraham begins in Genesis 22:2: **"Take now thy son, thine only son Isaac, whom thou lovest, and get thee into the land of Moriah; and offer him there for a burnt offering upon one of the mountains which I will tell thee of."** Here was Abraham's second chance. Abraham was determined to please God this time by believing His word alone. God wanted to see (or rather let Abraham see for himself) whether Abraham loved Him supremely and chiefly above all else. Many of us want Abraham's faith but not Abraham's trial. And yet it is not so much our faith but the *trial* of our faith that is **"much more precious than of gold that perisheth" (I Peter 1:7).**

Our writer says that Abraham was **"tried."** In Genesis 22:1 we read that Abraham was **"tempted."** Temptations come in two kinds: (1) those that spring from Satan or from natural causes, and (2) those of which God is the architect. The first kind of temptation is described in detail in James 1:13-15. In this case, God is clearly not the author.

The second type of temptation, however, is better termed a **"proving,"** or **"testing,"** rather than a temptation. God is behind this, and He certainly took the whole responsibility for what He ordered Abraham to do. When God tries us in this manner, it is a wonderful sign that He is dealing intimately with us. When this happens, it is absolutely impossible to tell whether it is more aptly to be called a blessing or a trial.

Abraham's trial was of two sorts—emotional and spiritual. The emotional aspect was having to do to his own *flesh and blood* what God had told him to do. The spiritual side was having to do to the child of promise what God had told him to do. Which sort of trial was harder for Abraham to bear I would not quibble over, but the writer of our epistle emphasizes the spiritual side. He that **"had received the promises"** offered Isaac, **"Of whom it was said, That in Isaac shall thy seed be called" (Hebrews 11:18).**

It made no sense that God should have Abraham do away with the only link between himself and posterity. As for the emotional side of the trial, which the writer of Genesis especially emphasizes, God identifies with Abraham's feelings. **"Take now thy son, thine only son Isaac, whom thou lovest."**

God knew how dear Isaac was to his father. And yet, if we get too attached to something or someone, we may well be in danger of losing them. As for the spiritual side, Abraham's having to cut the only tie between promise and fulfillment might have tempted him to argue with God: "Surely not. You said, "Count the stars," and if I slay Isaac, there will be no stars to count. *No way,* God!" But Abraham didn't argue.

You may say, "God promised to use me; all I have is this (or that) gift, and if I abandon it, God cannot use me." I answer: The best you have to offer must be abandoned to God for His purposes. Let God decide what He will use. That which God may see in you may be quite different from what it is you think God is after. He doesn't want your gift. He wants You. When you are utterly and totally His, then what you have to offer becomes subsidiary.

The Five Principles of Testing

There are five principles that lie behind Abraham's ordeal:

1. *When God is testing us, that which He asks of us often makes no sense at the time.* If it made complete sense, there would be little need for faith. The Word of God comes to us from beyond the level of human understanding and thus transcends human reason. By removing the props that give support to a completely rational mind-set, God tests us to see whether we will believe His Word alone. God's order to give up Isaac made no sense at all.

2. *Faith is never perfected (brought to maturity) without going through suffering.* When James used Abraham as an illustration of justification by works, he added, **"Seest thou how faith wrought with his works, and by works was faith made perfect?" (James 2:22)** Saving faith is given to us not for the purpose of salvation only, but also that we might become the manner of persons that flesh and blood alone cannot produce. Saving faith is therefore given to us also that it might develop into experimental faith. But it never comes apart from suffering. Even Jesus was made perfect **"through sufferings" (Heb. 2:10; see also Heb. 5:8)**. Paul exhorted that **"we must through much tribulation enter into the kingdom of God" (Acts 14:22).**

3. We must obey the Holy Spirit without knowing all the details or implications of His will. Abraham's failure to pass the first test, which resulted in the **"son of haste,"** consisted in the fact that he was not content not to know all the implications of God's promise. When God tested Abraham this time, He told him to offer Isaac **"upon one of the mountains which** *I will tell thee of"* **(Gen. 22:2).**

Abraham might have been tempted to strike a bargain with God: "First tell me where this is leading me." Our trouble is often that we want God to give us all the details now. We must be willing not to know the end from the beginning (as God does). Jesus said, **"He that is faithful in that which is** *least* **is faithful also in much" (Luke 16:10).** Sometimes God gives us a general idea what He is doing but keeps the details in reserve so as to test our obedience one moment at a time.

4. We may not be permitted to let anyone else know what God is doing with us. **"Abraham said unto his young men, Abide ye here with the ass; and I and the lad will go yonder and worship, and come again to you" (Gen. 22:5).** It is often a severe temptation to share with at least one other person what God is saying to us. I do not say there are not times when one should do this, especially with one of very mature judgment. But often God brings us to such a lonely place that there is not one soul who would understand, even if you told all that is in your heart.

Abraham refused to "cast the pearl before the swine" (his servants), for sometimes the **"swine"** is not an unbeliever. Neither did Abraham tell Isaac what he was up to. There are two kinds of **"swine"**: non-Christians, who can never hope to understand, and Christians, who sometimes still cannot understand. Matthew 7:6 points to one of the most difficult principles to be learned in the Christian life.

5. The worst suffering may lie yet in the future (it almost always comes just before the end of the test). Has not Abraham had enough suffering by now? He has consented to obey God's order, but is there yet more suffering? There is. **"And Isaac spake unto Abraham his father...Behold the fire and the wood: but where is the lamb for a burnt offering?" (Gen. 22:7)** You might ask, "How could Abraham stand that?" I don't know. This aspect of the story has always seemed to me to be the most painful.

But if your suffering becomes what you would have thought was almost unbearable, it is a good sign—a very good sign—*on one condition*: you don't murmur. If you murmur, the whole trial will be aborted and God's blessing will be postponed (who knows for how long?). Abraham was being tested now to the full. Would he murmur? Would he shake his fist at God and shout, "*Why?*" No, Abraham simply said, **"My son, God will provide himself a lamb for a burnt offering: so they went both of them together" (Gen. 22:8).**

We are told that Abraham **"stretched forth his hand, and took the knife to slay his son" (Gen. 22:10),** for Isaac was **"as good as dead" (Heb. 11:12).** Abraham was now carrying through outwardly what he had committed himself to inwardly. Abraham had in his heart of hearts said "good-bye" to Isaac.

By the way, Abraham had to *do* it. He had been willing, yes. But he had to *do* it. Our hearts are so deceitful. We often think we are willing, but when it comes to *doing* we tend to play games with ourselves. When Abraham stretched forth his hand, there was not the remotest thought that God would stop him. Many of us know the ending of the story and often fancy a happy ending of our particular trial along the lines of the Abraham and Isaac story.

We say to ourselves, therefore, that we are willing. We are *willing* to abandon ourselves to God—but do we *do* it? We are willing to obey; but do we *do* it? Jesus said, **"For whosoever will save his life shall lose it; but whosoever shall lose his life for my sake and the gospel's, the same shall save it" (Mark 8:35).** As long as we are thinking of saving our lives the whole time we are trying to lose them, it manifestly shows we haven't abandoned ourselves yet. To lose oneself is to carry out outwardly what we are committed to inwardly, without any thought of a happy consequence.

Don't try to predict the end from the beginning. What God will salvage when you offer your own body a **"living sacrifice" (Rom. 12:1)** is His business. You will say, "But there will be nothing left of me for Him to use." When there is nothing left of you for God to use, you are at that moment finally ready to be used.

Chapter Fourteen

Sons of Promise

Hebrews 11:18-19

Of whom it was said, That in Isaac shall thy seed be called: accounting that God was able to raise him up, even from the dead; from whence also he received him in a figure.

Our examination of the above two verses leads us to some of the most sublime principles to be found in the whole of Christian thinking. I am sometimes tempted to regard Hebrews 11:19 as the most profound verse in the New Testament. I admit that it is a verse which is a bit difficult to grasp, but the reward for doing so is almost dazzling. Truth like this comes through suffering. **"The secret of the Lord is with them that fear him; and he will shew them his covenant" (Psalm 25:14).** God wanted to show Abraham His secret, but it could not come without immense suffering.

The secret to which all Christians are called is that of making the transition from the flesh to the Spirit. It is always a painful transition. The time came when Jesus prepared His disciples for a realm beyond the fleshly level, and they didn't like what they were hearing one bit. **"It is expedient for you that I *go away*,"** Jesus told them after noting that, **"Because I have said these things unto you, sorrow hath filled your heart" (John 16:6-7).**

Abraham needed a lesson in how to make the transition from the human level to the level of the Spirit. That was the whole purpose in the ordeal of having to sacrifice Isaac. When God initially said, **"In Isaac shall thy seed be called" (Gen. 21:12),** far more was meant than Abraham could have known. That word seemed merely to mean that the promise referred to Isaac's seed, not Ishmael's. Sarah had said to Abraham, **"Cast out this bondwoman [Hagar] and her son [Ishmael]: for the son of this bondwoman shall not be heir with my son, even with Isaac" (Gen. 21:10).**

Abraham found that word extremely hard to take: **"The thing was very grievous in Abraham's sight because of his son" (Gen. 21:11).** At that stage Abraham simply took all this to mean that the promise (see Gen. 15:5) would be fulfilled through Isaac's posterity rather than Ishmael's. And even this was most painful for him to bear. But that was only the beginning. Far more than that was entailed in the words, **"In Isaac shall thy seed be called."**

The Natural Seed vs. the Spiritual

What was not disclosed in these words was *how* Isaac's seed would be called. Abraham needed to be taught how the offspring of Isaac would be incorporated into the family of God. Abraham needed to be taught the nature of God's calling of His people. It had seemed to Abraham that his **"seed"** would be continued by procreation, just as Isaac was born. Although Isaac was a "miracle baby," he was nonetheless born naturally. Surely Isaac's children and his children's children would be born like anybody else. But Abraham was to receive a lesson not only in the nature of God's calling, but also in what was meant by **"seed."**

What Abraham was to learn, and what the writer of the Epistle to the Hebrews brings out, is precisely what the Jews seemed never to understand about Abraham's seed. **"We be Abraham's seed,"** they retorted proudly to Jesus (John 8:33). These Jews would have been most annoyed that **"seed"** should mean something other than that which was continued by procreation alone. For these Jews took Genesis 21:12 (**"In Isaac shall thy seed be called"**) simply to mean the exclusion of Ishmael's line.

The Apostle Paul, however, claimed that those who did not embrace God's promise showed that they were in fact sons of Hagar—no matter what they may have been in terms of racial extraction (see Gal. 4:21-31). This meant that, according to Paul's allegorical use of Hagar and Sarah, Jews who didn't accept the gospel of Christ revealed their spiritual origin as traceable to *Hagar*.

Likewise, according to Paul, Gentiles who believed the gospel revealed their spiritual ancestry as traceable to Sarah. It is only the spiritual origin that ultimately matters. "For they are not all Israel, which are of Israel: neither, because they are the seed of Abraham, are they all children...that is, they which are the children of the flesh, these are not the children of God: but the children of the promise are counted for the seed" (Rom. 9:6-8).

One can see from Paul's interpretation of Abraham's seed in Galatians 4:21-31 why the Jews found Paul's theology so revolting. Imagine Paul calling a Jew an Arab! But, says Paul, a Jew is a son of Ishmael if he remains under the Law and refuses to embrace God's promise. This interpretation of Paul has great relevance at the present time. I speak particularly of those of the Islam religion, which is largely comprised of sons of Ishmael. If the offence to the Jew is to be told, he is a spiritual son of Ishmael if he is not emancipated from Sinai, so the offence is equally to the Muslim when he realizes that the gospel makes him a spiritual child of Isaac! In both cases one must make the transition from the human level to the level of the Spirit.

Abraham learned all of this hundreds of years before Paul. This is precisely our writer's point in Hebrews 11:19, that Abraham received Isaac **"in a figure."** The command to Abraham to sacrifice Isaac was God's way of teaching Abraham that the continuity of his seed was to be at a spiritual level—regeneration not procreation. This is why the writer of our epistle is concerned with the spiritual rather than the emotional side of Abraham's trial. The emotional aspect was that Abraham had to show that he loved God more than Isaac; the spiritual aspect was that Abraham must abort the continuity of the natural seed.

THE PRINCIPLE OF DISCONTINUITY

Abraham's ordeal, then, was far more than a trial of his faith; it was to demonstrate the radical discontinuity between the natural level and the spiritual (supernatural) level. To illustrate: If there were automatic continuity between the natural and spiritual, then all the children of Isaac would be regenerate by birth (It would follow that all children of Christian parents to the present day are regenerate by natural birth). But Abraham was to learn that what God meant by **"seed"** was spiritual not physical.

The only way to teach Abraham this was for him to give up Isaac utterly. Abraham must kill Isaac and see him no more. The writer of the Epistle to the Hebrews tells us that Abraham was willing to go through this ordeal if only because he knew that God could raise Isaac from the dead. In any case, Abraham bade his son a final farewell and lifted his hand in the air with a sharpened knife—when suddenly the angel grabbed Abraham's arm in the nick of time. God stepped in, and Abraham never forgot it.

Abraham got Isaac back. But Isaac never looked the same again. Abraham got Isaac back **"in a figure."** Abraham was now detached from his son at a natural level. The tie ever afterwards was spiritual. He learned that his **"seed"** was to be continued not at the level of the flesh, but by God's own intervention. Jesus' way of putting it was, **"Ye must be born again" (John 3:7).**

God did not want Isaac to continue by nature. God wanted Isaac's existence to be due entirely to the intervention of the Spirit. Thus, Isaac's posterity would be after the **"figure"** of Isaac—not the Isaac who lived before God's intervention at Mount Moriah. The Greek word translated **"figure"** is *parabole*—a parable, a likeness pointing beyond itself, or a figure. Corrie ten Boom tells us that after leaving Ravensbruck prison, it was like being snatched from death. After that her life was not her own, because she should have been dead. That is precisely the way Abraham regarded Isaac after the ordeal at Moriah. But most important was Abraham's discovery that his seed would be continued only by God's own intervention.

Abraham's offspring, unless given faith by God's stepping in, would not be regarded as his due **"seed."** The seed would continue by regeneration not procreation. Abraham's true posterity would be reckoned as having sprung from the **"figure"** of Isaac, not the Isaac before the sacrifice. All of Abraham's posterity, who do not undergo a similar death and intervention by God's act, are reckoned to be sons of haste who have Hagar for a mother (even if they can trace their ancestry straight back to Isaac!).

God is determined to keep the responsibility for the continuation of the seed of Isaac to Himself alone. He lets nature perpetuate itself according to the laws of creation and procreation. This, of course, is also by God's sovereign will. But it is His will in nature only. His act of creation and His purpose in redemption are not rendered identical by His decree (otherwise, regeneration is universal, and the command **"Ye must be born again"** is nonsense).

In His secret will, God has claimed total responsibility for the continuation of Isaac's seed. The angel of the Lord called to Abraham **"the second time, and said, *By myself* have I sworn, saith the Lord, for because thou hast done this thing, and hast not withheld thy son, thine only son: that in blessing I *will bless thee*, and in multiplying I will multiply *thy seed* as the stars of the heaven"** (Gen. 22:15-17).

What matters, then, is the **"figure"** of Isaac not the **"flesh"** of Isaac. We are sons of Isaac only if we have been raised to new life. **"Except a corn of wheat fall into the ground and die, it abideth alone: but if it die, it bringeth forth much fruit. He that loveth his life shall lose it; and he that hateth his life in this world shall keep it unto life eternal"** (John 12:24-25). Isaac owed his survival to God alone, not to his father Abraham. And so with all of us. The flesh must be put in subjection before the Spirit can reign; nature must die before grace can rule.

Perhaps the chief folly of the modern church is its confounding of nature and grace. If the secret work of the Holy Spirit were completely withdrawn from the visible church today, I suspect that it would largely continue as if nothing had happened. The church was never intended to be continued by procreation, neither was it meant to continue by natural means.

The "calling" of Isaac's seed is by God's own act. This means a radical discontinuity between nature and the work of the Spirit. One wonders how many there are in the modern church who haven't a clue what the nature of this call is. **"Abraham, Abraham."** God always calls so that we know it is His voice and does so in a most intimate fashion. **"Fear not, for I have redeemed thee, I have called thee by thy name, Thou art mine"** (Isa. 43:2). **"My sheep hear my voice, and I know them, and they follow me"** (John 10:27).

Continually Empowered by the Spirit

What is grace today so often drifts into human effort tomorrow, all because one assumes continuity without God's intervention. The second generation of an apocalyptic movement, or reformation, or awakening often tends to be perpetuated by human strength rather than by the power of God. What began in the Spirit often seeks perfection in the flesh. Look at many denominations today which were born by God's direct ownership and anointing in a previous generation, but which bear little resemblance to former days. The same is true with colleges, Bible colleges and seminaries— even Christian unions in universities, industries and governments.

We must never presume that God's approval yesterday ensures His blessing upon an institution today. But it is this very presumption that has allowed the modern church to become worldly and indifferent to the need for fresh power from on high.

Calvin claimed that the true church is present if there are three things in force: (1) the Word of God is preached, (2) the sacraments are administered, and (3) discipline is exercised. I should like to add a fourth: that the vast difference between human exertion and the activity of the Spirit be understood and reverenced. This would mean that one could not take for granted that the presence of the Spirit is in the church merely because the first three items are adhered to.

Surely Calvin's three points can be carried out from generation to generation without the fresh intervention of the Spirit. This is precisely why Jesus warned the church at Ephesus that the lampstand could be removed from its place (Rev. 2:5). Surely this would ensure the great

Reformation principle *ecclesia reformata sed semper reformanda*—"the church reformed but always to be reformed."

God wanted to establish the principle of discontinuity between the flesh of Isaac and the **"figure"** of Isaac. Abraham's sacrifice of Isaac was the original demonstration of "the church reformed but always reforming." It not only helps ensure that the Spirit will be present in the church, but also that every conversion will be a miracle. The "calling" of Isaac's seed is when God "steps down"—indeed, stoops down to where we are. God is concerned about His witness in the world and never wants His witness abandoned to nature.

The genius of my old denomination can be detected in the words of its founder Phineas Bresee, who would shout to his anointed fellow-ministers, "Keep the glory down." That was in the early part of this century when that particular denomination—born in revival—was just getting started. Bresee knew that their only hope was the presence of God. He knew that if the Spirit departed, that denomination had no other hope.

It is the Spirit alone that makes men **"sons of promise."** Left to themselves they will be **"sons of haste."** All men are sons of haste by nature. **"Behold, I lay in Zion for a foundation a stone, a tried stone, a precious corner stone, a sure foundation:** *He that believeth shall not make haste"* **(Isa. 28:16).**

Chapter Fifteen

The Faith
of Isaac

Hebrews 11:20

By faith Isaac blessed Jacob and Esau concerning things to come.

We have noted that the Genesis account of Abraham and Isaac deals more with the human side of things, whereas the writer of the Epistle to the Hebrews is entirely concerned with the spiritual. It can be said of the Old Testament and the New Testament generally, that the latter gives us spiritual insight into the former. In the case of Isaac however, the human side is not very gripping. Genesis reveals him as a rather unexciting, if not passive, man.

· The frequent mention of Isaac's name can be misleading if one thinks that he was a powerful man himself. He was not. One is tempted to say that a spiritual interpretation of Isaac is about all our writer could have found in him in any case. His extraordinary birth is about Abraham and Sarah; his miraculous deliverance is about Abraham; when it came to choosing a wife, he had nothing to do with it (Abraham ordered his servant to do it all).

Thus when we read that Isaac did anything **"by faith,"** we may well wonder how the writer was able to see such a thing! For even this was not carried out apart from the mischievous manipulations of his wife Rebekah. We may ask, was Isaac ever his own man? It would seem at first that Isaac never did anything of his own free will.

This is precisely the point that our writer wants us to grasp: Isaac is an example of the overruling grace of God. A spiritual interpretation of Isaac is really our only option. But what can be said about him as an historical individual? First this, that he never broke out of his father's mold. He repeated his father's sin when he told Rebekah to say to Abimelech that she was his sister (Gen. 26:7; Gen. 20:2). He also repeated his father's financial success (Gen. 26:12), but all this was only a continuation of a powerful father's influence. He had a strong father, a protective mother (Gen. 21:10), and eventually a domineering wife! And yet this account should encourage anybody who knows what it is like to be completely upstaged by those who by nature are more powerful and clever.

On the other hand, to continue Abraham's seed—at the level of the Spirit—was no insignificant thing to do. All that Isaac was ultimately supposed to do, he did. Abraham had been one of the great men of all time, and it was not likely that his son Isaac could match his father's achievements—nor were they needed. Isaac would do well to be faithful to his calling. It takes a truly great man to be faithful to God's calling without trying to be another "original."

The curse of the modern ministry is the need to be clever and make a name for oneself. Isaac did what he had to do, and when he had to do it, he did it well. When his wife Rebekah was barren, he prayed effectually to God, and she conceived (Gen. 25:21). God's covenant with Abraham was renewed with Isaac as well (26:24), and Isaac built an altar and called on the name of the Lord (v. 25).

Gaining the Blessing by Trickery—and Faith

When Rebekah conceived, it turned out that there were twins in her womb. The Lord said to her, **"Two nations are in your womb, and two peoples from within you will be separated; one people will be stronger than the other, and the older will serve the younger" (Gen. 25:23—NIV).** The key words were, **"the older will serve the younger."** Esau and Jacob were born—in that order. Esau was the clever hunter who pleased his father. Jacob was the "homebody," who pleased his mother. **"Isaac loved Esau, because he did eat of his venison: but Rebekah loved Jacob" (Gen. 25:28).**

One day Esau came in from hunting, exhausted and hungry. Jacob happened to be cooking a stew, and Esau asked for some. But Jacob agreed upon one condition only—that Esau would sell his birthright. Esau was tired and famished and rationalized, "If I don't eat, I will die, so what good is my birthright anyway?" Clever Jacob pulled this one off in brilliant fashion: Esau sold his birthright. What was a birthright? It was a position of honor and prestige that came *naturally* to the male child who first opened the womb. The eldest child was to receive double the inheritance of the others. In the Hebrew tradition the eldest child also got the father's blessing, an event of no small consequence.

What follows is perhaps the most remarkable account in the Bible of the free will of man working simultaneously with the eternal, unchangeable will of God. A most difficult theological concept to grasp is the reconciliation of the sovereignty of God and the will of man. C.H. Spurgeon said that these two lines are like those of a railway track which are parallel on earth but which will meet in eternity. J.I. Packer's use of the word "antinomy" in his book *Evangelism and the Sovereignty of God* is most helpful. An antinomy is defined as two parallel principles that are irreconcilable but both true. Dr. Packer points out that, theologically speaking, the sovereignty of God and the will of man only *appear* to be irreconcilable.

If we can live in this tension, we will be mature Christians. In any case, the account of Rebekah's manipulations illustrates how man is free; but the promise of Genesis 25:23 **("The older shall serve the younger")** illustrates the foreknowledge and sovereignty of God. Rebekah overheard the aged and blind Isaac ask Esau to make him some **"savory meat"** that he might give Esau his blessing before he died (Gen. 27:4-5).

Rebekah secretly ordered Jacob to fetch two young goats that she might prepare them for Isaac just the way he liked. She also had Jacob put on Esau's clothes so that when the old man felt him, he would think it was indeed Esau. The situation was touch and go for a few moments as Isaac sensed something was not quite right (Gen. 27:22), but in the end, after

Jacob had lied to his father (v. 24), Isaac gave Jacob the cherished blessing (v. 27). Thus Jacob, the younger son, got what he wanted.

That is not the end of the story, however. Within a few moments in came Esau with the venison his father had requested. A terrible shock came to the old man. **"Who are you?"** Isaac asked. **"I'm your son Esau, your firstborn,"** came the reply. **"Isaac trembled very exceedingly"** and reported to Esau that the blessing had already gone to Jacob—**"yea, and he shall be blessed" (Gen. 27:33).** When Esau heard those words, he **"cried with a great and exceeding bitter cry, and said unto his father, Bless me, even me also, 0 my father" (v. 34).**

Esau managed to squeeze out a blessing, but there was not much joy to be had from it. Whereas Jacob's blessing was this—**"Let people serve thee, and nations bow down to thee...cursed be every one that curseth thee, and blessed be he that blesseth thee" (Gen. 27:29).** Esau's blessing was less than glorious. **"And by the sword shalt thou live, and shalt serve thy brother; and it shall come to pass when thou shalt have the dominion, that thou shalt break his yoke from off thy neck" (Gen. 27:40).**

Our verse tells us that what Isaac did, as related above, he did by faith. **"By faith Isaac blessed Jacob and Esau concerning things to come."** The obvious question is: where does faith come in? The answer is that Isaac refused to change what he had done. In faith Isaac blessed Jacob, even though he thought it was Esau; and when Isaac found out that it was Jacob not Esau, he stuck to his guns. The proof of this is not only in his remarkable statement—**"yea, and he *shall* be blessed"**—but in the inferior blessing he bestowed upon Esau.

Isaac believed that what he had pronounced upon Jacob would stand, because he believed in the authority that was his as God's instrument. Although Esau was naturally the firstborn, Jacob was the firstborn spiritually. That Isaac did not reverse his blessing was a sublime act of faith; it showed that he knew how the seed of his father Abraham was to be continued—at a spiritual level.

What Isaac did, then, was to ratify by faith what had been foreknown by God's decree. When the twins were still in Rebekah's womb, God told her something of His secret will. When the Apostle Paul in Romans 9 was arguing precisely the same point that our writer to the Hebrews has made, he cited the account of the twins in the womb. **"For the children being not yet born, neither having done any good or evil, that the purpose of God according to election might stand, not of works, but of him that calleth; It was said unto her, The elder shall serve the younger"** (Rom. 9:11-12).

Paul in fact derived three doctrines from the story: (1) the doctrine of election **("that the purpose of God according to election might stand")**; (2) the doctrine of justification by faith **("not of works")**; and (3) the doctrine of regeneration **("but of him that calleth")**.

This is exactly what our writer meant when he said, **"By faith Isaac blessed Jacob and Esau concerning things to come."** For Isaac by faith affirmed (1) God's choice of Jacob instead of Esau; (2) God's blessing of Jacob though he did not deserve it; and (3) the continuity of his seed at a spiritual not a natural level—regeneration not procreation. Had Isaac operated according to the flesh, he would have reversed his blessing, demanded that Esau be rewarded and Jacob punished, and set an unchangeable precedent that the firstborn is to inherit God's grace no matter what. But his magnificent affirmation, **"Yea, and he (Jacob) shall be blessed,"** is essentially the same thing as when Isaac himself was given back to Abraham **"in a figure."**

It is this very kind of thinking and discernment that shows a spiritual mind at work, and explains why our writer graces Isaac's stance with the title **"faith."** When old Isaac said to Esau his firstborn, "You are too late— I have given my blessing to Jacob," it was his finest hour. He may have lacked the color and magnitude of stature of his father Abraham, but when it came to doing what he was supposed to do, he did it—and he did it well.

The Will of God and the Will of Man

What emerges primarily from the account of Isaac's faith, then, is the lesson that the nature of faith is to give priority to the will of God over man's will. We know that Isaac preferred Esau to Jacob (Gen. 25:28), but he acted not according to his natural inclination but according to a higher principle. An integral part of bearing the cross is acting upon this higher principle rather than a principle that is commensurate with human affection.

It is not an easy thing to do. It is exactly what Abraham had to do when he gave up Isaac. Now Isaac himself was having to do the same with Esau. Surely nothing is more painful.

All of us know the pain of having to make decisions that hurt those that are closest to us. It is the supreme test whether we value God's honor more than the reciprocal appreciation that comes when we please those we naturally want to please. An illustration of this very principle is the story about G. Campbell Morgan when it came to naming his successor at Westminster Chapel. Dr. Morgan had such stature that anybody he chose would probably have been accepted almost uncritically by the people. Many thought he would select one of his sons, but he didn't. He followed a higher but also more painful principle.

So much recommending of ministers to churches today is strictly according to the flesh, and the consequence often is that men are elevated beyond the level of their competence (if only spiritual competence). **"Humble yourselves therefore under the mighty hand of God, that he may exalt you in due time" (I Pet. 5:6). "For promotion cometh neither from the east, nor from the west, nor from the south. But God is the judge: he putteth down one, and setteth up another" (Ps. 75:6-7).**

Behind Isaac's faith, however, was the sovereign will of God. Isaac acted with integrity and with the most admirable kind of courage. But underneath this painful stance lay God's predestination. We may not naturally like this matter of predestination, but to despise it is to despise God. At the bottom of the story of Isaac blessing Jacob is the fact that God had told Rebekah in advance, **"The elder shall serve the younger." "As it is written, Jacob have I loved, but Esau have I hated" (Rom. 9:13; Mal. 1:2-3).** When Isaac blessed Jacob and Esau **"concerning things to come,"** he was only affirming God's secret decree. Faith ratified what God had foreordained.

It is not to be denied that many proponents of the doctrine of predestination have come up with a very hard and rigid (not to mention unbalanced) understanding of this teaching. Predestinarians may have done more damage to the doctrine of predestination than all the anti-predestinarians in the world. They have turned thousands right off the teaching by their unhappy defenses of it and, in some cases, by their ungodly lives.

But in the end, *everyone*—some sooner, some later—must confess the truth God put to Moses, **"I will have mercy on whom I will have mercy, and I will have compassion on whom I will have compassion" (Rom. 9:15; see Exod. 33:19).** I like the way the founder of my old college, J.0. McClurkan, put it. He said, "Work at it like an Arminian, then rest in it like a Calvinist." Rebekah and Jacob appear to have been pretty good "Arminians"!

True greatness in the end, however, is seen in old Isaac. This ordinary man earned a place in the "faith chapter" of the Bible by doing one thing: acting in faith at the right moment. He was strong in the end. That is what made him great. What makes a small man is trying to be great. Shakespeare said that "some are born great, some achieve greatness and some have greatness thrust upon them." Isaac was born great, and had greatness thrust upon him. But he achieved greatness only one way; by faith.

Chapter Sixteen

THE FAITH
OF JACOB

Hebrews 11:20

By faith Jacob, when he was a-dying, blessed both the sons of Joseph; and worshipped, leaning upon the top of his staff.

One of the interesting things concerning the eleventh chapter of the Epistle to the Hebrews is the way our writer's mind works. For example, it is interesting that he is selective not only with regard to Old Testament personalities but also with regard to the events by which these stalwarts are known. Admittedly, in the case of Isaac there was not much choice in demonstrating his faith. But in the case of Jacob, it would seem there were several events that show his faith, and certainly events that are better known than that of his **"leaning upon the top of his staff"**!

Jacob's faith could surely be more vividly described in connection with his vision of the ladder (Gen. 28:12-22), or the painful encounter with Laban (Gen. 29-31), or most certainly his wrestling with the angel at Peniel where his name was changed to Israel (Gen. 32:28). But our writer passes by these better-known stories and comes up with an account that most of us would not have thought to take so seriously.

Why should our writer select this particular event? Is it because it is an event that continues the theme of the discontinuity of the natural seed of

Abraham? Partly, yes. But why mention Joseph? Was not the greater promise tied to the tribe of Judah (Gen. 49:8-12)? Why then, if our writer is
going to give but one verse to Jacob in this illustrious chapter, does he
select this event? The answer to this question will occupy a good deal of
this chapter.

Our writer centers on an event which Jacob himself had come to think
would never take place. It is an event which followed Jacob's deepest grief,
but one which showed the highest kind of joy. It is a demonstration that
sorrow can be turned into joy, and yet this would never have been possible
but for the marvelous providence of God. When the writer of the Epistle to
the Hebrews seized upon this event, he not only showed the heartbeat of
Jacob himself but put his finger on the pulse of what makes faith *faith*.

Sorrow Turned to Joy

Jacob had twelve sons, who came to be known as the twelve tribes of
Israel and, eventually, simply Israel. Of the twelve sons Joseph was Jacob's
favorite. This is partly why our writer put Joseph's name in verse 21. Since
Joseph was the son of his old age, Jacob loved him more than any of his
other children. Accordingly, Jacob made him a **"coat of many colours"**
(Gen. 37:3).

It is a bit surprising that Jacob should show partiality like this, for he
himself knew what it was like not to be his father's favorite. Children tend
to imitate their parents for good or ill. Many times a parent will vow not to
treat his children as he or she had been treated, but more often than not
the same bad conduct or habit tends to be passed on.

When Joseph's brothers realized more and more that their father preferred Joseph, this made them more and more jealous. And yet this
jealousy was intensified because of a certain gift which had been given to
Joseph, one which Jacob could not have had anything to do with: the
knack of having dreams which seemed to be predictive in nature. Joseph
may not have been especially wise to reveal such dreams to his brothers.
He should have known this would not help his relationship with them—
but he did.

One day Joseph told this dream to them, **"We were binding sheaves in the field, and, lo, my sheaf arose, and also stood upright; and behold, your sheaves stood round about, and made obeisance to my sheaf"** (Gen. 37:7). His brothers did not need a lot of perception to get the interpretation, **"Shalt thou indeed reign over us? or shalt thou indeed have dominion over us?"** The consequence was that his brothers **"hated him yet the more for his dreams, and for his words" (Gen. 37:8).**

The eventual result was that they decided to slay him. One of the brothers (Reuben) suggested that they merely cast him into a pit in the wilderness and let him die. But Judah overruled, thinking it unwise to **"conceal his blood."** Instead, they decided to sell Joseph to the Ishmaelites (see Gen. 37:26-27). The brothers kept his coat, dipped it in blood and laid it before Jacob, who instantly concluded that **"an evil beast hath devoured him" (Gen. 37:33)**—the very conclusion the brothers had hoped for.

Our verse (Heb. 11:21) tells us that Jacob, when dying, blessed both the sons of Joseph. Obviously the above is not the end of the story of Joseph. I shall bring in the details about Joseph in the next chapter. The ultimate consequence was this: Joseph, having been made the governor of Egypt, sent for his eleven brothers and old Jacob. Thus, when our writer tells us that Jacob blessed Joseph's sons, it was an event Jacob had never expected to see—a time of unspeakable joy.

Our writer tells us that Jacob **"worshiped."** Indeed he did. Jacob had much to be thankful for. In his old age he witnessed not only the reunion of his sons, but more importantly, the external confirmation of God's promise to him.

It had seemed that his twelve sons had come to a disintegration that was beyond repair. **"I will go down into the grave unto my son mourning,"** Jacob rashly vowed (Gen. 37:35). But he was not mourning now. When he was told the whole truth regarding Joseph, he held no grudges. **"It is enough; Joseph my son is yet alive: I will go and see him before I die" (Gen. 45:28).** When Jacob was dying, he had the privilege of blessing Joseph's two sons, and he **"worshiped."**

It will be recalled that the internal confirmation is prior to the external confirmation; the inner testimony of the Spirit is primary. But once the external confirmation comes in the context of what God had promised would take place, such outward confirmation brings unspeakable joy. For we live in the real world, a world of sense perception: We see, smell, feel, taste, and hear. When our senses witness what God promised would be true, it brings great joy indeed. God delights in doing this for us. That is precisely what old Jacob was enjoying upon his death bed. It came none too soon. But it was soon enough.

Jacob's leaning upon his staff suggests reflection as well as the need for physical support. Worship is partly reflection. One reflects upon the promises of God and also the fulfillment of these promises. There comes a time that we need to see the actual display of the goodness of the Lord in the land of the living (see Psalm 27:13). Faith leads to *visible* answers to prayer. Jacob could now reflect on a full life—and what a life that had been!

Manipulation and Guilt

Jacob had reason to look at his own life as one of failure. He not only knew great sorrow; he knew himself to be, as it were, the world's greatest manipulator. Everett Shostrom in *Man the Manipulator* describes the person who exploits, uses, or controls himself and others in self-defeating ways. Manipulation is the opposite of what Abraham Maslow would call self-actualization.

My own definition of manipulation is man taking control of things as opposed to letting God do things His way. Manipulation is pulling, striving and standing in the place of God lest He not act as we think He should! The manipulator often experiences considerable guilt for his exploits. Jacob had to live with himself over his act of manipulating Esau to sell his birthright. Could what happened to Joseph be God's punishment for what Jacob had done to Esau? Jacob may well have had that thought a thousand times.

All of us, when something happens that is tragic or almost unbearable, tend to accuse ourselves. When our faith wanes a bit, a frequent tendency is to forget God's greater purpose and begin to suppose that we have done something to miss His will.

Jacob may also have compared himself with his father and grandfather and judged himself to be manifestly unworthy of his heritage. Abraham by now was a legendary figure; Isaac, though not a spectacular man, had been a good man, and Jacob lived with the realization that he had deceived his own father. Jacob had more than one reason to feel great guilt and shame over the way he had lived his life. If Abraham's seed was to continue through Jacob, Jacob may have thought he had become a disgrace to the great tradition. When Joseph was apparently **"rent in pieces,"** we are told that Jacob **"refused to be comforted; and he said, For I will go down into the grave unto my son mourning"** (Gen. 37:33-35).

God let Jacob live in suspense until his last days. Our verse in Hebrews tells us that Jacob's happy reflection did not come till **"when he was a dying" (Hebrews 11:21 KJV)**. God did this with good reason. He had a great lesson for Jacob to learn. Some of life's greatest riddles are not solved until one's sunset years (and some not even then). Some of life's greatest mysteries are kept hidden from us for an indefinite period.

We tend to blame ourselves. But even that never helps matters. For blaming ourselves is a subtle form of manipulation; we tend to think that if we blame ourselves, we have beaten God to it, as it were. Guilt is often a defense mechanism by which we get a quasi-righteous feeling. Guilt makes some people feel better—so they tend to think. But no. Blaming ourselves— even if we were wrong—is self-centered if we do not turn the whole matter over to God.

Do you want to know the happiest news in the world? It is this: We are not held guilty for anything we did. Jacob learned precisely this lesson in his dying hour. God held him guilty for absolutely nothing. As for Joseph, he was in God's hands. Joseph would say to his eleven brothers: **"You meant evil against me, but God meant it for good"** (Gen. 50:20 NAS). And so with Jacob. In his dying hour the whole of God's purpose fitted together. His worship now was one of most happy reflection. The riddle was solved. God's greater purpose had been at work the whole time.

I should think it was a moment of unspeakable joy for the old patriarch to be able to look back and see the truth of what Paul the Apostle would later articulate: **"We know that all things work together for good to them that love God, to them who are the called according to his purpose" (Rom. 8:28).** Only God could do that. As for Joseph, not only was he himself preserved, but his preservation was the very preservation of the nation of Israel.

Mending a Broken Past

God can take our broken past and mend it so beautifully that it gives the appearance of being predestined in every way. God sanctioned Jacob's wicked past, saying, **"Jacob have I loved."** God not only sanctioned it, He owned it. In owning it He took the blame for it. In taking the blame for it He claimed to have caused it. In causing it He absolves all our guilt so that there is no way under the sun we could conceive of its having worked out any better—even if we ourselves had managed the whole matter from the beginning.

The glory of predestination is that God takes our wicked past and owns it—as though our folly was His idea. That does not always mean that it was His idea, but the past works together for good so brilliantly that it gives that appearance. God does not want us to feel guilty. Even Joseph did not want his eleven brothers to feel guilty.

Jacob's worshiping upon the top of his staff, moreover, was not only a happy reflection but a renewed conviction that God indeed had taken the responsibility to perpetuate the seed of Abraham. Thus Jacob, in his dying hour, was to discover what Abraham and Isaac had learned—that their seed at the natural level must have discontinuity. Jacob showed that he had finally learned that lesson. Making the transition from the flesh to the Spirit is the most difficult of all lessons to learn.

The proof that Jacob had learned this is that (1) he gave the greatest blessing to Judah, not Joseph; and (2) when he **"blessed both the sons of Joseph,"** he displeased Joseph in the way he did it. If Jacob had followed the path of his natural affection, he would have ensured that Messiah would come through the tribe of Joseph. Jacob's greatest blessing was to the one whose idea it was to sell Joseph into slavery. **"Where sin abounded, grace did much more abound"** (Rom. 5:20).

In blessing Joseph's sons—Manasseh and Ephraim—Jacob put his right hand on Ephraim and his left on Manasseh. Joseph objected and lifted old Jacob's hand off Ephraim's head to put it on Manasseh's. **"Not so, my father: for [Manasseh] is the firstborn; put thy right hand upon his head. And his father refused, and said, I know it, my son, I know it: he also shall become a people, and he also shall be great: but truly his younger brother shall be greater than he"** (Gen. 48:18-19). Old Jacob thus demonstrated he was in the great tradition of Abraham and Isaac after all. Our writer tells us that Jacob did what he did in this connection **"by faith."**

Our writer selected this event in Jacob's life to show that the patriarchs each had in common the conviction that their seed would not continue at the natural level. In the case of Jacob we can see that the old man, who had thought he would go to his grave in mourning—if only because he would not be able to bless Joseph—gave the greatest blessing to Judah. When Jacob got Joseph back, he blessed Judah. But he also blessed Joseph's sons—against his son's will.

Our writer's selection, then, supports his thesis concerning the nature of faith and the nature of Abraham's seed. It demonstrates that "all's well that ends well," but also that this is something that comes apart from manipulation. That was the lesson old Jacob was to learn. Did he learn it? Yes, he did. How do we know? Because what he did with reference to the sons of Joseph was carried out **"by faith."**

Chapter Seventeen

The Faith of Joseph

Hebrews 11:22

By faith Joseph, when he died, made mention of the departing of the children of Israel; and gave commandment concerning his bones.

A favorite story in the Bible for many is that of Joseph. To me none is as thrilling, uplifting and dazzling. **"How unsearchable are his judgments, and his ways past finding out!" (Rom. 11:33).** The story of Joseph is the best illustration of what William Cowper would later write:

God moves in a mysterious way,

His wonders to perform;

He plants His footsteps in the sea,

And rides upon the storm.

It is a pivotal story in Old Testament history. It shows how the children of Israel got to Egypt in the first place and further suggests that God wanted Canaan to be a land of promise in a way even the Patriarchs had not fully imagined. The story of Joseph is another reminder that God does not forget His own, that vengeance is His prerogative, and that what happens to us is transcended by His greater purpose. We often get preoccupied with our little world and tend to forget that we are in a battle between God and Satan. The story of Joseph is a reminder that, whereas what happens to us is important to God, the reason why all things work together for good is ultimately because God has a greater purpose in the world.

Our verse in this chapter makes us face again the way our writer's mind works. Of all the events in Joseph's life to select from, why this? Our writer wants us to see that Joseph, too, eventually saw things beyond the earthly realm.

Our verse shows us three things: (1) that Joseph forecast Israel's return to Canaan; (2) that in giving instructions regarding his bones Joseph identified himself with Canaan, not Egypt (showing where his true affections were); and (3) that all this was done **"by faith."** The purpose in this chapter is to focus upon the way in which Joseph was persuaded concerning Israel's future.

When it is stated that Joseph did what he did (in prophesying of Israel's future) **"by faith,"** it must be said that this act was but the culmination of Joseph's life of faith as a whole. Had not God so miraculously guided Joseph himself, he would not likely have been so sure of what he was predicting. When God deals with us in an extraordinary way, it is meant to encourage us that something even more extraordinary is yet to come. God works in an extraordinary manner with those he has a greater purpose for.

When Joseph reflected upon his own life and could see that all that had happened to him was ultimately for the good of Israel, he had no difficulty believing that the same God would continue to take care of His covenant people. Thus, when we can look back on our lives and can see God's unmistakable hand in sparing us, blessing us, preserving us and guiding us, it should tell us all we need to know about our future. **"He which hath begun a good work in you will perform it until the day of Jesus Christ"** (Phil. 1:6).

The Purpose of Suffering

Although Joseph's ending is happy and holy, there is little that is either happy or holy about its beginning. Joseph was sold into slavery because of **"envy"** (Acts 7:9). Indeed, in the beginning of this story nobody is justified and all are at fault in some way. Jacob played favorites (Gen. 37:3). Joseph poured fuel on the fires of family jealousy by telling his dreams (Gen. 37:5). The brothers then acted out their jealousy (Gen. 37:27-28). Our verse (Hebrews 11:22) shows a triumph of godliness, but that is at the end of Joseph's story.

When Joseph was sold to the Ishmaelites, it thrust him into hard, physical work—something he knew nothing about. For his father had let the other sons do the hard work. Joseph had been born with a silver spoon in his mouth. His new life certainly made up for that deficiency! He was now a slave. The Ishmaelites in turn sold him to Potiphar, an officer of the Pharaoh in Egypt (Gen. 39:1). **"But God was with him,"** Stephen reminded the Sanhedrin (Acts 7:9).

Joseph was made the master of Potiphar's house. Soon Joseph faced a new kind of trial—sexual temptation. Potiphar's wife was certainly not the virtuous woman described in Proverbs 31:10. She made an attempt to seduce Joseph, but failed. He retained his morality and rejected her (Gen. 39:12). "Hell hath no fury like a woman scorned." Potiphar's wife claimed that Joseph made improper advances towards her, and he was put in a prison dungeon.

Joseph's stay in prison was no doubt the lowest point in his life. God had promised to bless him and exalt him (see Gen. 37:9), but where was the promise of that now?

His purposes will ripen fast,

Unfolding every hour;

The bud may have a bitter taste,

But sweet will be the flower.

Joseph had some company in prison: the king's butler and the king's baker. One morning each of them revealed a dream he had had the night before. Joseph interpreted the dreams, and his interpretations were per-fectly fulfilled. The butler was released in three days and the baker was hanged. Joseph had made a request to the butler (just before the latter was restored to his old position), that the butler would tell Pharaoh about him (Gen. 40:14). That slight attempt to manipulate Providence did not work, however: **"Yet did not the chief butler remember Joseph, but forgat him" (Gen. 40:23).** Humanly speaking, then, Joseph had no hope at all.

When God deals with a man in an extraordinary manner, He almost always puts him through unusual suffering. The essence of that suffering is often the bleakness of the future. What makes suffering *suffering* is the complete absence of hope, humanly speaking. God chastens those He intends to use in an unusual way by bringing them right to the edge of despair. This way they can never question the explanation for their deliverance when it comes.

> Blind unbelief is sure to err,
>
> And scan His work in vain;
>
> God is His own interpreter,
>
> And He will make it plain.

Humanly speaking, there was absolutely no hope for Joseph. Even if Potiphar himself believed in Joseph (which he might well have done—or Joseph would hardly have gotten off with just a prison sentence), he could not release him; he had to save face.

God had a way of exalting Joseph. But there was no way of predicting before the event how it would come about. It was the combination of several things: perfect timing, Pharaoh in trouble, and Joseph's old gift of interpreting dreams. Pharaoh had a dream for which Joseph alone had the interpretation. The butler came in handy after all, but he would have remembered Joseph even if Joseph had not asked to be remembered.

If our gift is authentic, it will be recognized at the right time—with or without our trying to ensure its use. When Pharaoh's own interpreters failed to interpret the dream, the butler remembered Joseph. What made the butler remember Joseph was not Joseph's anxiety, but the dearth of gifted and godly men on the horizon at the time. God was preparing Joseph for such a time as this. There was no way of rushing this moment.

Joseph's interpretation not only pleased Pharaoh, but because it ensured Egypt's wealth and glory for many years to come, Joseph was made governor of Egypt as a reward for his interpretation and wisdom. The dream of Pharaoh showed that there would be seven years of plenty (during which time Egypt should store food) followed by seven years of famine (when other nations would come to Egypt to buy). Joseph therefore was made second only to Pharaoh himself in Egypt. He had come a long way from that cold, dingy dungeon.

Becoming a Man of God

Joseph had also come a long way from Canaan. And now, after the seven years of plenty the famine came; all the world was affected by it, including Canaan. In a short period of time old Jacob said, **"I have heard that there is corn in Egypt" (Gen. 42:2),** and sent ten of the sons (all except Benjamin, who had replaced Joseph as the father's favorite) to Egypt to buy grain. Any foreigner had to go to the governor first, so here came these ten men to Joseph. Joseph recognized them, but they didn't recognize him. Joseph was dressed in different garb, in the meantime had learned Egyptian, and spoke to them through an interpreter. He was not entirely devoid of a feeling of revenge, for he gave them a rough time for a while and made them sweat (see Gen. 42-44).

Eventually Joseph revealed himself to them, weeping openly, **"I am Joseph; doth my father yet live?" (Gen. 45:3).** The result was that the eleven brothers and their wives brought old Jacob down to Egypt to live; for the famine was destined to last a while longer. The children of Israel were made elite visitors in Egypt, having been given the land of Goshen (Gen. 47:6). Joseph was personally vindicated, a vindication which included the fulfillment of his dream.

But personal vindication was not Joseph's concern. When Jacob died, the brothers were terrified. They were certain that Joseph would at last get even for their wicked crime against him. They **"fell down before his face" (Gen. 50:18)** which is about as literal a fulfillment of Joseph's dream as one can imagine. But a "new" Joseph emerges. **"Fear not: for am I in the place of God?" (Gen. 50:19).** The vindication which he once craved he now eschewed. Vindication, or vengeance, meant absolutely nothing to Joseph now. When he wanted it, he couldn't get it; when he didn't want it, he got it. **"For whosoever will save his life shall lose it: and whosoever will lose his life for my sake shall find it" (Matt. 16:25).**

The writer of the Epistle to the Hebrews describes the "new" Joseph—Joseph in a figure, as it were. Joseph had indeed come a long, long way; it was a greater distance than from the dungeon or from the land of Canaan. It was from the flesh to the Spirit. Joseph no longer lived at the level of natural human responses. Thus he said to the brothers: **"But as for you, ye thought evil against me; but God meant it unto good, to bring to pass, as it is this day, to save much people alive"** (Gen. 50:20).

Joseph's personal vindication was swallowed up by a greater concern for the kingdom of God. He lost sight of vengeance and gained the victory that matters. The "new" Joseph no longer cared for what he had thought was so crucial—his personal feelings.

Had Joseph followed his natural feelings, he would have wanted to get even. Not only that, he would have been at home in Egypt. For Egypt had become a happy place in which to live. He was second only to Pharaoh, and he could have had a tombstone that portrayed forever all he meant to Egypt. For Joseph was Egypt's hero, and Pharaoh made no attempt to hide it. Furthermore, all his brethren and their wives, seventy in number (Gen. 46:27), were enjoying security and prestige in Egypt.

But when Joseph was dying, he had two things on his mind: the exodus of Israel from Egypt and his own bones. He knew that Israel did not belong in Egypt. Moreover, he wanted to ensure that his bones would be carried with them when they departed. For he had not been at home in Egypt.

Joseph, then, was motivated by the same concern as the earlier patriarchs. That is why our writer included Joseph in the "faith" chapter, and that is why this particular event was selected. **"And Joseph said unto his brethren, I die: and God will surely visit you, and bring you out of this land unto the land which he sware to Abraham, to Isaac, and to Jacob. And Joseph took an oath of the children of Israel, saying, God will surely visit you, and ye shall carry up my bones from hence"** (Gen. 50:24-25). Joseph thus disclosed where his treasure was. Jesus said, **"For where your treasure is, there will your heart be also"** (Matt. 6:21).

Joseph had been a dreamer; now he was a prophet. He had been a braggart; now he was self-effacing. He had been the object of envy, for which there was a ready human explanation; now he manifested a concern and spirit that defied explanation on the human level. He had become a true man of God.

God had been with Joseph all along. In that sense, he had always been a man of God. But God was preparing Joseph for far more than all Joseph could have projected. When he was in the dungeon, he simply wanted out. But God had much more in mind for him than a mere release from prison. Many of us have ambitions that, in their carnality, are way, way short of what God has in mind for us. **"Eye hath not seen, nor ear heard, neither have entered into the heart of man, the things which God hath prepared for them that love him" (I Cor. 2:9).**

Little did Joseph know what he was being prepared for. But in the end his chief concern was the future of the kingdom of God and his identification with it—even with those who had betrayed him. For the vision of the greater glory of God caused his personal feelings to disappear.

Chapter Eighteen

MOSES'
PARENTS

Hebrews 11:23

By faith Moses, when he was born, was hid three months of his parents, because they saw he was a proper child; and they were not afraid of the king's commandment.

Moses was the greatest figure in the Old Testament. The whole of the Old Testament may be said to revolve around Moses as the New Testament does around Jesus Christ. **"For the law was given by Moses, but grace and truth came by Jesus Christ" (John 1:17).** Our writer now turns from Joseph to Moses, and in doing so brings in the tribe of Levi. Up to now he has shown that the seed of Abraham is continued by a spiritual intervention, and whatever else this shows, it demonstrates the unpredictability of God's way of showing His glory. **"For who hath known the mind of the Lord? or who hath been his counsellor?" (Rom. 11:34).**

And yet it is hardly surprising that our writer should bring Moses into this "faith" chapter of the Bible. Moses gets seven verses. While Abraham in a sense was given more attention, our writer was more interested in discussing the nature of faith than the personality of Abraham. He focuses upon Moses as a person, but still more so as a man of faith.

There is a sense in which we will learn more about the theology of the writer of the Epistle to the Hebrews than we will about Moses. This has been quite true already. For our writer is not intending to tell us anything these Hebrew Christians did not know about the personalities of these great people; he is showing that faith is not a New Testament innovation. In fact, he is showing that there is really nothing new to be known about faith. These godly people experienced it thoroughly long before the gospel of Jesus Christ appeared.

It is a sobering indictment of us Christians if we who have the fulfillment of the promise are inferior in faith and godliness to those who did what they did under the mere **"shadow of good things to come" (Heb. 10:1).** If they did what they did, how much more should we excel? That is a central theme of the entire Epistle to the Hebrews: **"How much more...?"**

Our writer introduces Moses by referring to his birth. The birth of Isaac was dealt with (v. 11); now the birth of Moses is mentioned. What makes Moses' birth extraordinary is not the promise of that birth, but the melancholy atmosphere surrounding it and his miraculous preservation in the light of this atmosphere. But the most consoling thought that emerges is the watchful care of our Heavenly Father over His own. We often tend to think that God has forgotten us, especially if events in the world create an atmosphere charged with wickedness and utter unbelief.

The story of Moses should remove all doubts as to God's care and concern for His own. For when we are not thinking about God, He is still thinking about us; the things which concern us concern Him. Our concern for Him is intermittent and vacillating; His concern for us is constant and steady. In fact, our very concern and keen desire to see His face can only be explained in terms of His secret work in us. He always makes the first move, even though He often is pictured as reluctant to respond to our cry. Our very calling upon His name is the consequence of His enabling power to do so.

The writer concludes that what lay behind Moses' parents hiding the little baby was nothing other than faith. He believes that the only explanation to be given for what Moses' parents did was faith. However, although it is called faith, it is remarkably different from any faith described in Hebrews 11 up to now. First of all, it wasn't Moses' faith at all (despite the wording **"By faith Moses"**). Secondly, there was a distinct limit to that faith: it only held out for three months. But these things provide yet another lesson for our encouragement and comfort.

Adversity Initiates Spiritual Progress

For approximately a hundred years the children of Israel enjoyed both prosperity and prestige in the land of Goshen, the portion of Egypt designated by the Pharaoh who exalted Joseph. Pharaoh proclaimed, **"I will give you the good of the land of Egypt, and ye shall eat the fat of the land" (Gen. 45:18).** Pharaoh was eternally grateful to Joseph, whose godly gift made Egypt a nation of wealth and splendor.

But Joseph died. So did his brothers and **"all that generation" (Exod. 1:6).** In the meantime the children of Israel **"were fruitful, and increased abundantly, and multiplied, and waxed exceeding mighty; and the land was filled with them" (Exod. 1:7).** At this point in the Book of Exodus there emerges one of the most ominous texts in all of Holy Writ—Exodus 1:8: **"Now there arose up a new king over Egypt, which knew not Joseph."**

As long as Joseph was alive—indeed, as long as the same Pharaoh was alive—the children of Israel did fine. They had a free ticket in Egypt's land of Goshen. And yet that may have been a root of their subsequent problem. It seems likely that they would have been quite content to stay in that land indefinitely. We read of no indication (or the slightest hint) that any of the children of Israel felt it was time to return to Canaan, although Joseph's last words to them pointed to the transitory nature of Egypt. As long as they were being fruitful and were in security and ease, they obviously postponed to a later generation any notion of pulling up stakes in Egypt. After all, Egypt was home to the children of Israel. Why should they leave?

How many of us would never make spiritual progress unless we were driven to our knees by some adverse change of circumstances? Most of our spiritual attainments can be dated by some melancholy change of atmosphere (perhaps near catastrophe) that made us turn to God as we had not been doing. Chastening, God's negative work of sanctification, is the only word most of us hear. We must learn to be thankful for the Pharaoh **"who**

knew not Joseph." For, however unpleasant, he becomes God's instrument for our salvation.

On the other hand, this ominous change of events for the children of Israel symbolizes how a nation—even a church or religious institution—tends to forget the secret of her greatness. Egypt owed her wealth to the children of Israel. Jesus described the church as the **"salt of the earth" (Matt. 5:13).** The nation of Egypt was indebted to Israel. So is the world today. **"Blessed is the nation whose God is the Lord" (Psalm 33:12).**

The irony in the Western world in recent years is how the church is being almost completely forgotten. **"Righteousness exalteth a nation: but sin is a reproach to any people" (Prov. 14:34).** Thus also with a church or religious institution; a change of leadership that emerges from a generation that **"knew not Joseph"** often scoffs at and overturns the very principle that made that original movement what it was.

And yet the new Pharaoh may be the only thing that will ultimately ensure that the people of God are driven to their knees to call on the name of God as they should do. This new Pharaoh was threatened with the prospect that the children of Israel would outnumber the Egyptians, so he enslaved them and put them to hard work. **"The Egyptians made the children of Israel to serve with rigour: and they made their lives bitter with hard bondage, in mortar, and in brick, and in all manner of service in the field" (Exod. 1:13-14).**

That is not all; it was ordered that every son born into the house of Israel should be killed. **"But the midwives feared God, and did not as the king of Egypt commanded them, but saved the men children alive" (v. 17).** The result was that **"Pharaoh charged all his people, saying, Every son that is born ye shall cast into the river, and every daughter ye shall save alive" (v. 22).**

That is the world into which Moses was born, and that is the context of Hebrews 11:23. Moses was born into a generation that was being threatened with utter extinction. Where is the God of Abraham, Isaac and Jacob now? God had made a promise to Abraham: **"Count the stars...so shall thy seed be,"** but things were looking very bleak indeed. But when God appears to have forgotten His people, one may be sure that He is hard at work preparing for the preservation of His church.

God Overcomes our Weak Faith

The situation described in Exodus chapter 1 has arisen many times since, and is an apt description of things in many parts of the world at the present time. God however is hard at work to preserve His people. Though God may come at an unexpected time and in an unexpected way, He is never too late and never too early. He's always just on time.

A fair baby was born—**"They saw he was a proper child,"—"A goodly child" (Exod. 2:2).** He did not come through the tribe of Joseph (as one might have predicted—if God was going to raise up a deliverer) or the tribe of Judah (who got the greatest blessing from old Jacob). Moses was born into the house of Levi, whose blessing from Jacob was shared by Simeon's tribe and was a blessing that gave no hint of a future hope for Israel (see Gen. 49:5-7). **"Can there any good thing come out of Nazareth?" asked Nathanael about Jesus (John 1:46).** God delights in doing the unexpected, the unpredictable and overturning laws of probability.

Every parent thinks his baby is **"goodly"** and **"proper,"** but Moses' parents were right! They knew indeed that this baby was different. They managed to hide baby Moses for three months. We are told that this was done by faith. It was not Moses' faith. Faith is conscious and precipitates activity; Moses was a passive, helpless infant.

The faith described in Hebrews 11:23 was the faith of Moses' parents generally and his mother particularly. Our verse says **"parents;"** the original account in Exodus speaks only of Moses' mother. Obviously it was both. Yet it was an incongruous faith; it was rather strange and uncharacteristic of the faith we have seen up to now in Hebrews 11. For Moses' parents acted in faith not knowing exactly *why.*

What precipitated this faith? At the natural level it was Moses' actual appearance. This shows that God can use outward things to attract, to encourage, and even to stimulate belief. Thus, as a witness to the world, one must not forget this. Paul said, **"I am made all things to all men, that I might by all means save some" (I Cor. 9:22).**

Sometimes what appears as a very human or fleshly motivation is really the hidden work of the Spirit. When such is the case, we are unlikely to be conscious of what is taking place; the Spirit is self-effacing and secret, but He lies behind it all. This is also why there is such a thing as a vicarious, perfect faith that lies beyond our weak faith. **"Likewise the Spirit also helpeth our infirmities: for we know not what we should pray for as we ought: but the Spirit itself maketh intercession for us with groanings which cannot be uttered" (Rom. 8:26).**

Although Moses' parents acted in faith not knowing why, the proof that it was faith indeed is that **"they were not afraid of the king's commandment."** This is sufficient evidence that faith is the right name for their activity. Faith is a *persuasion,* and persuasion cancels fear. **"Thou wilt keep him in perfect peace, whose mind is stayed on thee: because he trusteth in thee" (Isa. 26:3).** They had every reason to be afraid. But they weren't. Why? They were persuaded that God was at work with regard to this child.

However, this faith was short-lived. It only lasted three months. **"When she could not longer hide him, she took for him an ark of bulrushes, and daubed it with slime and with pitch, and put the child therein; and she laid it in the flags by the river's brink" (Exod. 2:3).**

Perhaps a stronger faith would have brought Moses up in that household? Who can deny that God could have continued this "faith of three months" for an indefinite period? But three months was the limit to their faith. God does not ask us to impute to ourselves more faith than is there. We don't have to pretend or "prove to God" that we are strong when we are not. Their faith lasted three months. No more. The time was up. They knew it.

But their limited faith was still strong enough to turn Moses loose on the River Nile. They knew that the same God who gave him could keep him. They knew God would continue to protect a child like that. They didn't know exactly what was happening, and they weren't sure why they were doing it.

They reached the point where they had to turn their baby completely over to God—something every parent must do in any case. They knew that if they were right in thinking God had given them an extraordinary child for an extraordinary mission, the same God would take care of him.

What made them turn Moses loose? Answer: They did it when the fear that had been absent was threatening to come in if they kept Moses at home any longer. For three months they were not afraid. But now they were beginning to be afraid.

We sometimes feel guilty that we have no more faith than we have. We often start out strong; in midstream we switch our course because we feel weak. The Apostle Paul recognized this. None should **"think of himself more highly than he ought to think; but to think soberly, according as God hath dealt to every man the measure of faith" (Rom. 12:3).** It is not a sign of weakness to admit to it; it is strength.

When we get to heaven, we shall not only see that our weak faith was made up for by the strength and faith of our Lord Jesus Christ; we shall see, as Moses' parents eventually did, that the limits of our faith fit perfectly into God's ultimate plan.

Chapter Nineteen

Moses' Self-Identification

Hebrews 11:24

By faith Moses, when he was come to years, refused to be called the son of Pharaoh's daughter.

We have observed more than once that our writer does not intend to tell his readers anything new about the figures he chose to write about—only that these men did what they did because of their faith. For this reason the writer of the Epistle to the Hebrews makes casual references to the events, as if the reader knew the circumstances backwards and forwards. In other words, he wrote to those who were very familiar with the Old Testament. Are we? The Epistle to the Hebrews will make little sense generally if we are not, and this is also true with regard to the famous men of Hebrews 11. We therefore must be sure we have a certain knowledge of the persons and events as we move along in this great "faith" chapter of the Bible.

When our writer refers to Moses' having **"come to years"** then, it is assumed that we know all that had happened to Moses in the meantime. It will be recalled that Moses was turned loose on the Nile by his mother when he was but three months old. What happened was this: Pharaoh's daughter **"came down to wash herself at the river; and her maidens walked along by the river's side; and when she saw the ark among the flags [reeds], she sent her maid to fetch it. And when she had opened it,**

she saw the child: and, behold, the babe wept. And she had compassion on him, and said, This is one of the Hebrews' children" (Exod. 2:5-6).

Moses' older sister had been keeping an eye on the ark, and when she observed that Pharaoh's daughter wanted to keep the baby, she volunteered to find a nurse for him. The result was that Moses' own mother became the nurse until such time as the child was to be returned to the house of Pharaoh. It was Pharaoh's daughter in fact who gave the baby his name. **"And she called his name Moses: and she said, Because I drew him out of the water" (Exod. 2:10).**

We have seen already that it was the faith of Moses' parents that lay behind his being hidden for three months until they turned him loose on the Nile. We must not underestimate the importance of his parents' faith. For although their faith was only good for three months in the sense of keeping him hidden, this faith was confirmed by the fact that they were given the child right back in a few hours' time—under the official sanction and protection of the government!

By the time when they had to give their son to Pharaoh's daughter, their own influence upon the child had been vast and profound. Moses would grow up in Egypt with an Egyptian mother, in an Egyptian culture and in an Egyptian atmosphere; but he had one thing going for him no other Egyptian child had: the prayers of godly parents. What can be more important than this?

Although Moses' parents had to part with their son much sooner than is normal or desired, they regarded him as a child given by God. They regarded him as "on loan" from God as long as they had him. They no doubt committed him to God and prayed for him after they said good-bye. We must never underestimate the value and advantage of Christian training; neither should we underestimate the prayers of Christian parents once that child has left home—at whatever age. I am sure that Moses was committed to God by his mother every day.

Moreover, the world into which Moses was thrown had every conceivable disadvantage insofar as the worship of the true God is concerned. In the first place, Moses was turned loose into the same river that meant death to every other Hebrew boy. Many of us as parents tremble as we bring up our children in a world of wickedness into which, sooner or later, they shall be thrust. Moses' mother planted a kiss on the cheek of her three-month-old son and laid him among some papyrus reeds on the river Nile, never expecting to see him again.

There is a sense in which every Christian parent must do this. We must ourselves die not only to sin and the world, but to our children as well. They are God's creation (not ours), and we must give them back to God, abandoning them to His care.

Moses' Egyptian Identity

The likelihood of Moses ever embracing the God of Abraham, Isaac and Jacob was made virtually nil by the pagan education he would receive. There would be no catechism, no rehearsal of the great Hebrew tradition, no stories about Abraham, Isaac and Jacob—not even of Joseph and how his ancestors happened to be in Egypt. **"And Moses was learned in all the wisdom of the Egyptians, and was mighty in words and in deeds" (Acts 7:22).**

Moses became an expert in astrology, Egyptian science, Egyptian philosophy, Egyptian history, and the Egyptian language. He had an Egyptian world-view. Moses was Egyptian in nearly every possible way. This is not exactly the kind of training one would expect to prepare a future leader of the children of Israel. This should encourage all of us who worry about our children and their future. "For with God nothing shall be impossible" (Luke 1: 37). "How unsearchable are His judgments, and His ways past finding out!" (Rom. 11:33).

Our verse states that Moses, **"when he was come to years, refused to be called the son of Pharaoh"s daughter."** We do not know at what age a child comes to "accountability" (as it is sometimes called), when a child is utterly responsible for himself. Some say ten, some say twelve, some fifteen, some eighteen.

Frankly, I think it is an insoluble dilemma. Any answer to the question is sheer speculation. What we do know is this: Moses, when he came of age, found himself. He discovered his true identity. According to Stephen this happened when Moses was about forty years of age—rather late in life to come to oneself! **"And when he was full forty years old, it came into his heart to visit his brethren the children of Israel"** (Acts 7:23).

This suggests that Moses' parents waited a good while before they got their prayers answered. Some Christian parents regard themselves as failures if their children aren't mature saints at the ripe old age of eighteen. We must remind ourselves that, if we truly turn our children over to God, we must trust the same God to carry out His purpose in them. (By the way, stop and consider how patient God has been with *you*!)

Moses' faith matured at about the very time one normally settles into a permanent sense of security. Most of us want to feel settled and rather secure by the age of forty. Moses certainly had all the security in the world, humanly speaking, one could wish for. He was the grandson of Pharaoh, learned in Egyptian ways, and was mighty in words and deeds. This is not the sort of insecurity that motivates one to switch careers or change jobs or professions, much less is it what inspires a man to start life all over again. "Life begins at forty," it is often said; such was certainly true with Moses!

Instead of settling into Egyptian luxury and security, this man Moses began to feel a certain restlessness of spirit. He became more interested in his true identity than he was in fame and fortune. Faith causes this. Faith transcends the normal course of events. **"By faith Moses, when he was come to years, refused to be called the son of Pharaoh's daughter."** This faith manifested itself in Moses' rejection of his imposed identity.

His Egyptian identity had been superimposed upon him without his consent. When Pharaoh's daughter saw the baby crying in the little ark, she exclaimed, **"This is one of the Hebrews' children"** (Exod. 2: 6). How did she know? Moses, like all Hebrew males, had been circumcised. Egyptian babies were not.

Little Moses grew up knowing he was different from other Egyptian boys. There was no way this identity could be kept from him. The time came when he got utterly tired of his Egyptian culture and imposed heritage. This restlessness of spirit began to transcend his earthly security. No doubt Moses felt a secret affinity with those Hebrew slaves in the land of Goshen for years and years. He may well have had a battle within his own mind.

"Those are my people out there in Goshen," part of him said.

"But I am secure and at ease here in this palace," another part of him would argue.

"Those are my people."

"I am secure here."

The Turning Point

When he was fully forty, Moses came to grips with the matter. When he did so, he was never the same again. **"He refused to be called the son of Pharaoh's daughter."** **"He refused."** He rejected the identity that had been imposed on him. This rejection of an Egyptian identity our writer calls **"faith."** Moses' faith was very like that of his parents. They were acting in faith not knowing why they were doing what they did. He was acting in faith, and yet he could not have known all that was meant in the overthrow of his Egyptian heritage.

Regeneration always begins as an unconscious work of the Spirit. We do things but don't know why we are doing them. Consciously, we may feel motivated by what seems natural and earthly. Perhaps Moses' first sight of his people was but a human sympathy, even as his own self- awareness may have been. This is why many Christians go for a long time thinking that their decision to become a Christian was entirely their own. And in one sense it is entirely our own decision. But it is the maturity of grace and knowledge that leads one to see the hand of God behind all that we did— even though it seemed to be utterly in our own power.

The first evidence of faith in Moses, then, came not at Sinai, nor at the back of the desert, nor at the burning bush. It came when his heart was persuaded to visit his brethren. This is what led him to renounce his imposed identity. Faith always works this way: (1) his heart was persuaded; (2) his will was affected.

Although Moses' faith was not refined or well defined, it was a true faith. All of us are born with an imposed identity that we did not ask for. We are born in sin. We did not ask to be created. But we grew up in sin and learned to love it. It is by grace that we recognize—in Augustine's words:

"Thou hast made us for Thyself; our hearts are restless until they find their repose in Thee."

Paul said: **"I am the least of the apostles, that am not meet to be called an apostle, because I persecuted the church of God. But by the grace of God I am what I am: and his grace which was bestowed upon me was not in vain; but I labored more abundantly than they all: yet not I, but the grace of God which was with me" (I Cor. 15:9-10).**

Do not underestimate the natural affection Moses would have felt for his Egyptian mother—Pharaoh's daughter. She was the only mother he ever knew. He left his natural mother when he was a year old or, at the most, two years of age.

Pharaoh's daughter was "Mommy" to Moses, which shows that Moses felt the pain of parental disapproval. It was his first big test, and yet, compared to the suffering he would know later, it was that which was **"least"** (see Luke 16:10). But he passed that test. Whatever the temptation he felt at the age of forty to live in the luxury of the king's palace, whatever pain he felt in saying good-bye to his Egyptian mother, Moses passed this test.

It was his first test. It wouldn't be his last. But neither would he find any subsequent test more difficult, given the circumstances at that time.

But he passed. By faith.

Chapter Twenty

Moses' Choosing To Suffer

Hebrews 11:25

Choosing rather to suffer affliction with the people of God, than to enjoy the pleasures of sin for a season.

In the last chapter we observed the beginnings of Moses' faith. Regeneration is always unconscious at first, but it invariably results in a conscious decision. It begins in the heart, first unconsciously then consciously, but ends with the will. Moses was learned in all the wisdom of the Egyptians, but when he was fully forty years old, **"it came into his heart"** to visit his people. Faith led to action (as it always does); he decided to identify with his brethren (Acts 7:23).

Our verse in the present chapter elaborates on the same event, that of refusing to be called the son of Pharaoh's daughter. It tells us in actual fact what Moses *anticipated* when he made this decision to identify with his own people. In other words, Moses knew that great suffering lay ahead. It was painful to abandon the king's palace; it was painful to dissociate himself from his family in Egypt. Thus, in Hebrews 11:25 our writer tells us that Moses thought he was fully aware of the consequences when he chose to identify himself with the children of Israel. He chose to suffer affliction with the people of God as opposed to enjoying **"the pleasures of sin for a season."**

There is to be seen in this verse an illustration of the shock that comes, sooner or later, to all people of true faith. Although we may reckon ourselves willing to suffer, we are never quite prepared for the kind of suffering God may have in mind for us. Such suffering is as shocking (or surprising) as it is painful. We have seen that every generation has its stigma by which the believer is tested. We are now to see that every believer has his "shock" by which his earnestness is tested. Implicit in this discussion moreover is the issue of what is sound evangelism.

There are two extremes: (1) *Easy believing, when the cost of faith is completely disguised.* The new believer is told that he is going to heaven but is told nothing about discipleship—the lordship of Christ, the bearing of the cross, and persecution; (2) *The one-sided emphasis upon duty, so that the believer is sometimes diverted completely from Christ's death.* Such a believer looks at conversion entirely in terms of what he must give up and therefore misses the glory of Christianity—Christ as Savior, the nature of justification and Christian liberty.

A balanced message of the gospel will assure men of their readiness for heaven apart from works but will equally prepare them for the suffering which all believers must anticipate. The more superficial the preaching that leads to a conversion, the greater will be the shock when suffering comes. In any case, a shock to some degree comes to all, no matter how well they were prepared by the preaching.

We don't really know what precipitated Moses' faith. There was no evangelistic campaign in Egypt; there were no "Hebrew" tracts infiltrated into the king's palace that might encourage somebody to make his calling and election sure. As far as we know, the only vehicle the Lord used was Moses' conscience, and two things which may have arrested his conscience: his own circumcision (he knew he was different from other Egyptian boys) and watching his own people undergo gross mistreatment. It came into his heart to visit his people, and our writer tells us that it was a case of choosing to suffer affliction with them as opposed to enjoying the pleasures of sin.

And yet, Moses could not have known all that was entailed in that affliction. Stephen provides us with some of the details of Moses' suffering and tells us that Moses was to receive a severe shock. What was Moses' shock? Our writer tells us that it was suffering affliction **"with"** the people of God. But Stephen tells us that Moses' affliction was actually from or by the people of God. **"For he supposed his brethren would have understood how that God by his hand would deliver them but they understood not" (Acts 7:25).**

The most painful kind of persecution is often that which comes from within the family of God. Any family has secrets, and there are many secrets to be learned once a person is made a member of God's family. But the best-kept secret is the worst of all: that persecution often comes *from within the family.* None of us is prepared for that kind of suffering. Moses wasn't.

Moses intervened in a situation. He saw a fellow-Egyptian beating a Hebrew. Moses **"looked this way and that way, and when he saw that there was no man, he slew the Egyptian, and hid him in the sand" (Exod. 2:12).** Moses thought he would be cheered by the Hebrews. He thought he had surely endeared himself to them and that they would see that he was their friend. But they had the opposite reaction.

God's Shock Therapy

The deepest kind of shock awaits those who resolve to be totally resigned to God. God allows this shock for one simple reason: so that we will look to God alone and not be dependent upon any man. Moses thought he would get a bit of honor from the Hebrews. He was deprived of this. It hurt. But it was God's sovereign goodness and wisdom that prevented Moses from being nourished by the honor that comes from men. God is a jealous God. He wants us to look utterly and only to Him. Too often, that is a posture we take only after facing the shock of suffering.

We often tend to think that if we as Christians resolve to be more dedicated there will be a loud round of applause from everyone. But it seldom happens like that. For the very thing we think will confirm our obedience—namely, encouragement—is often withheld so we will get our encouragement from God. God wants our encouragement to be His joy. **"The joy of the Lord is your strength" (Neh. 8:10).** In the words of John Newton:

I asked the Lord, that I might grow
 In faith, and love, and every grace;
Might more of His salvation know,
 And seek more earnestly His face.

"Twas He who taught me thus to pray
 And He, I trust, has answered prayer;
But it has been in such a way,
 As almost drove me to despair.

I hoped that in some favoured hour,
 At once He'd answer my request;
And by His love's constraining power,
 Subdue my sins, and give me rest.

Instead of this, He made me feel
 The hidden evils of my heart;
And let the angry powers of hell
 Assault my soul in every part.

"Lord, why is this?" I trembling cried,
 "Wilt Thou pursue Thy worm to death?"
"Tis in this way," the Lord replied,
 "I answer prayer for grace and faith."

Moses had resolved in his heart that he would not be called the son of Pharaoh's daughter. This took great grace and courage. Surely God would reward him with an indisputable external confirmation? But no. Not yet. Suffering first. What kind? A shock. Moses supposed that they would understand that God by His hand would deliver them: **"But they understood not" (Acts 7:25).** Moses may have asked himself: "Is this the thanks I get for choosing to suffer affliction with the people of God instead of enjoying the pleasures of sin?" And yet this event, instead of being the beginning of the emancipation of the children of Israel, was really the beginning of Moses' own preparation.

Moses may have thought that rejection of his Egyptian identity was sufficient preparation. He may have thought that his turning his back on the pleasures of sin—luxury in the king's palace—was enough preparation. He may have thought his own name—the famous Moses who was Pharaoh's grandson—would make him the hero of Israel. He may have thought that his being learned in all the wisdom of the Egyptians, being mighty in words and deeds, was sufficient preparation. Moses chose to suffer affliction, yes. But he had no idea that there was suffering ahead far beyond anything he could have known. He anticipated the affliction. But not the shock.

Moses jumped the gun. Determined to take the deliverance of the children of Israel into his own hands, he resolved to identify with his brethren. Seeing an Egyptian mistreating a Hebrew brother, he took matters into his own hands; to him the great deliverance of the children of Israel was about to begin. He murdered a fellow-Egyptian. To Moses, this signaled that deliverance for Israel was at hand. Little did he know that such a deliverance was forty years away.

The very deed which he thought would endear him to his brethren only made them suspicious of him. The next day Moses saw two Hebrews quarreling, and Moses rebuked one of them. The reply came: **"Who made thee a prince and a judge over us? Intendest thou to kill me, as thou killedst the Egyptian?" (Exod. 2:14).** From that moment Moses was running scared; he said, **"Surely this thing is known" (Exod. 2:14).**

Not Yet Ready for Leadership

Whatever else this event proved, this much is certain: Moses was not yet ready for the leadership for which he was destined. As Dr. Lloyd-Jones once put it to me (the best advice he ever gave me): "The worst thing that can happen to a man is to have success before he is ready." Moses wasn't ready. Neither were the children of Israel. Preparation was needed on both sides. Moreover, what might have made Moses renounce his own decision to refuse to be called the son of Pharaoh's daughter was overruled. For his involvement in Israel's plight served to inexorably cut him off from Pharaoh. Moses might have said, "I've been a fool to leave the palace." But even if he had said that, it was too late. There was no way he could go back to the palace now. Moses was a wanted man. **"Surely this thing is known."**

God has a way of ensuring that His own purpose is not thwarted. He has a way of leading us to the place where we could not turn back even if we wanted to. He knows our frame. **"He remembereth that we are dust" (Psa. 103:14).** He knows how vacillating we might be. To ensure that Moses could not go back to the pleasures of sin, the word was out that he had killed an Egyptian. Moses was now on the run. **"Now when Pharaoh heard this thing, he sought to slay Moses. But Moses fled from the face of Pharaoh" (Exod. 2:15).** Moses was driven to godliness. All of us are congenitally allergic to godliness. We have to be driven to it. This is precisely why all the great saints have seen themselves as the greatest sinners.

Thus, any plan Moses may have had to return to the pleasures of sin was aborted by his own folly: killing an Egyptian. Although Moses' killing of the Egyptian was inexcusable, God nevertheless sovereignly used it to get Moses to the back of the desert. While there is no way we can excuse Moses for this heinous sin, it actually appears to be a stepping-stone in his career. The most profound truth to be learned from Romans 8:28 **("And we know that all things work together for good to them that love God")** is this: The fact that something worked for good doesn't mean that it was right at the time. For Moses' sin was very dangerous, in two ways: (1) It could have cost him his life; and (2) it could have destroyed the preparation that God had begun.

But God overruled any such outcome. This shows that God can use anybody. It shows that when a person makes a vow to suffer affliction with the people of God rather than to enjoy the pleasures of sin for a season, God tends to preserve him from utter extinction (although he may deserve extinction). The bent of Moses' life was to please God. There is a sense in which this alone saved him. God knew his heart. So God overruled. If Moses' Egyptian preparation seems incongruous for a future leader of Israel, so also was Moses' conduct: Murder is hardly the sort of thing anyone wants on his record. But when God is pleased to use a man, He is able to transcend the impediments that ordinarily disqualify him. In Moses' case the incongruity of his secular education and his ungodly behavior is outweighed by his resolution *to be what he knew he was*—a Hebrew, a child of God.

The knowledge of this outweighs any earthly pleasure. For earthly pleasures are, at best, **"for a season."** The knowledge that one is a child of God issues in a joy that lasts—forever.

Chapter Twenty-One

Moses and the Reproach of Christ

Hebrews 11:26

Esteeming the reproach of Christ greater riches than the treasures in Egypt: for he had respect unto the recompense of the reward.

The theme which our writer developed in Hebrews 11:24 is still continued in the above verse. We learn yet a little more concerning what was in the mind of Moses once he made the radical decision to leave Pharaoh's palace. Moses had anticipated that there would be **"affliction"** (v. 25) in his new role (although he was not prepared for all that entailed). In the present verse the writer states in a slightly different way what Moses perceived this affliction really to be. This **"affliction"** is now being called **"the reproach of Christ."** This verse is thus a further elaboration of Moses' original decision not to be known as the son of Pharaoh's daughter.

Indeed, Moses had not projected too accurately all that this affliction, or reproach, entailed. It was more complex than he had imagined. When a person becomes a Christian, he makes the most important decision in his life. But he cannot grasp all that is involved in this decision. Jesus says, **"Follow me,"** but we cannot possibly know all that this means. Moses was

quite certain that there would be hard days ahead as a result of his identi-
fying with his own people. But he did not know he would meet opposition
from the very ones he came to help.

And yet Moses realized that any suffering in God's will is still more
valuable than living for anything earthly. What kept Moses going was this:
He had respect for the **"recompense of reward."** That was his motivation.
Do not forget this: Moses needed motivation. There had to be something
to lure him away from the king's palace. One might ask, "What was in it for
Moses?" Surely he wasn't a fool. He was an intelligent man. He also had a
secure and attractive future. He was at the prime of life—aged forty. Something indeed was at the bottom of this extraordinary decision. Was Moses
being bribed? Had the elders of the children of Israel pooled their material resources and made Moses a financial offer that would equal what he
was getting as Pharaoh's grandson? What was in it for Moses? The answer,
says our writer, is simply that he had valued the **"recompense of reward."**
But what does this mean?

The Decision of Risk

In verse 25 our writer says that Moses **"chose"** to suffer affliction. In
verse 26 we are told that Moses **"esteemed"** a certain kind of reproach. Yet
surely, one would think, there was a great element of risk in this decision.
There is usually an element of risk in decision-making. We naturally want
the luxury of making a decision that is "risk-free" It is often put in terms of
"decision of safety" over against "decision of risk."

Some go by train rather than by air. Some prefer to walk than ride in a
car. Some put money in a bank; some buy stock. In the life and work of the
church, some give two per cent, or five percent, rather than their full tithe.
Some prefer the esteem of men to the stigma of following Jesus wholeheartedly.

But the extraordinary thing about Moses' decision was that there was
no material guarantee whatsoever that he was making the right decision.
In fact, this surely would seem a most absurd decision in terms of material
considerations. Consider that Moses was Pharaoh's grandson; he lived in
the luxury of the king's palace; he was an heir to the king's wealth; he
would never want for security and safety. And this our writer calls **"the**

treasures in Egypt." Had Moses lost his mind? Was this a mental break-down? Had his mind snapped?

We are told how Moses' own mind was working. **"For he had respect unto the recompense of reward."** This decision after all turns out to be the most pragmatic he could possibly have made. He set his affection steadfastly not upon Egypt's treasures but what our writer calls the **"recompense of reward."**

It was actually a very clever decision. It was astute and most prudent. It was brilliant. Moses' mind worked like this: Why try to win the battle when you can win the war? Life is the battle, but death is the war. This life (as we sometimes say) is a rat-race; it is dog-eat-dog—trying to get ahead and be seen with the best people.

What did Moses do? He cast his eyes upon the children of Israel. They were hardly the people to be seen with in terms of prestige and future promise. They were slowly being annihilated. Being seen with them would not make the front page of any newspaper. But Moses saw them as his brethren. More than that, he saw them as the **"people of God" (v. 25).** But still more important: Moses saw them as the *wave of the future.*

Moses could see in the children of Israel what nobody else could see. He could see that their ultimate inheritance would include inheriting the whole earth. Moses saw that behind those mistreated slaves in the land of Goshen was a God of purpose and design, not a God who is impotent or who works by chance. Moses saw that behind his **"brethren"** was a God of power, of providence and of purpose. To align himself with that God could not possibly be risky; to align himself with the God of Israel was to certainly win in the end.

The word our writer uses is *misthapodosian*—**"recompense of reward."** The Greek literally means **"reward for work."** However, it is not merely reward in terms of immediate payment or compensation—not "cash on the barrel-head" (as we would say in Kentucky). *Misthapodosian* is used here to denote a scheme of payment by *promise* of one whose fee is worth waiting for.

The recompense of reward is God's promissory note. It makes delayed gratification worth waiting for, whether it be in terms of vindication, or pleasure or riches. It is believing the promise that God will vindicate Himself and His people in the *eschaton*—the Final Day. Moses believed that. Refusing to be called the son of Pharaoh's daughter was the best deal he could imagine. He was getting out of that palace while the going was good.

SUFFERING SHAME FOR HIS NAME

The reproach which Moses esteemed, then, became a thing of beauty. "Beauty is in the eye of the beholder," it is often said. Non-Christians cannot understand why Christians would want to be Christians. Yet, the true Christian is a man or woman who feels quite the opposite, for they have been given to see what the natural man cannot see. Said Paul, **"We preach Christ crucified, unto the Jews a stumbling block, and unto the Greeks foolishness; but unto them which are called, both Jews and Greeks, Christ the power of God, and the wisdom of God" (I Cor. 1:23-24).**

What seems utterly absurd on the human level is utterly glorious and full of wonder at the level of faith. On one occasion the Apostles were physically beaten and censured. But they departed **"from the presence of the council, rejoicing that they were counted worthy to suffer shame for his name" (Acts 5:41).**

What is the essence of this reproach? It is three things:

1. *Solitude.* It is the awareness that you cannot get another person to see what you see (unless God shows it to him). As God loves everybody as though there were no one else to love, so every man who bears Christ's reproach loves God as though nobody else did. No one ever becomes a Christian unless he makes his decision in solitude.

2. *Silence.* This is the awareness that you cannot speak in your own defense. Christ, when He was reviled, **"reviled not again; when He suffered, He threatened not; but committed Himself to Him that judgeth righteously" (I Pet. 2:23).** There was no way that Moses could persuade the house of Pharaoh he was doing the right thing.

3. *Shame.* This is the awareness that you appear quite unattractive, perhaps disgraceful, in the eyes of people. The stand that you have taken is one that may make them furious. They will make you look and feel like a fool.

Moses **"esteemed"** this reproach! How much? He regarded this reproach as more valuable than the riches of Egypt! But why not? Asked Jesus, **"For what shall it profit a man, if he shall gain the whole world, but lose his own soul?"** (Mark 8:36). Moses' decision was the most pragmatic one that any man ever makes.

Some day, dear reader, you are going to die. What then? **"Take heed,"** said Jesus, **"and beware of covetousness: for a man's life consisteth not in the abundance of the things which he possesseth"** (Luke 12:15). **"Lay not up for yourselves treasures upon earth, where moth and rust doth corrupt, and where thieves break through and steal: but lay up for yourselves treasures in heaven, where neither moth nor rust doth corrupt, and where thieves do not break through nor steal"** (Matt. 6:19-20).

There is one more thing to be seen in our verse that we have not dealt with: This reproach is called **"the reproach of Christ."** How could that be? Moses lived almost fifteen hundred years before Jesus of Nazareth. How could it be called the reproach of *Christ?* Is this our writer's superimposing his own theology upon Moses? Partly, yes. Our writer did indeed superimpose the reproach of Jesus back upon Moses. But why? Because the reproach of solitude, silence and shame is not only universally true with the people of God, it also transcends time.

Reproach always has these three ingredients. Thus when Jesus came, He embodied the reproach perfectly in His person. He became the perfect example of the sort of persecution God's people have always had. It is called therefore the reproach of Christ—whether B.C. or A.D.

Yet there is more we ought to see about Moses' radical decision. He saw in this **"recompense of the reward"** a certain glory that motivated him to do what he did. I do not say that he physically saw the person of Jesus or that he would have called this reproach that of Jesus Christ. But I will say this: Moses was personally dealt with by the eternal Son of God when he made the decision he did. For Jesus Christ is **"the same yesterday, today, and for ever"** (Heb. 13:8).

Because it was our Lord who was dealing with Moses, we may be sure that Moses saw in this recompense of reward a **"figure"** so lovely and so powerful that it drew him out of Egypt with such persuasion and conviction that it became the easiest decision he ever made. Our writer simply gives this reproach the name which Moses saw in a figure—**"Christ."**

Hidden in the reproach of Christ is the greatest wealth of all: the joy of the Lord, His protective providence on our earthly journey, and heaven. Moses saw that. He had **"respect"** for it. Only a fool would have acted otherwise. It is not the fool who esteems the reproach of Christ more valuable than the treasures and pleasures of this life. It is the fool who doesn't.

Although Moses jumped the gun by thinking that the Great Deliverance for the people of Goshen was but hours away, the protective providence of our Lord more than compensated for the **"reproach."** Do not feel sorry for Moses at the back of the desert. The next forty years provided not only preparation, but some of the happiest years of his life. God supplied every need, even giving Moses a wife—Zipporah—and she gave him a son.

Those forty years provided a different kind of training. Moses needed rest from Pharaoh's pursuit, rest from the suspicion of the Hebrews, a time to think, and a time to know God more deeply. Moses was as much in the will of God keeping the flock of Jethro as he was when he received the Law on Mount Sinai. He enjoyed his preparation.

God's way is always the happiest way. The reproach issues in such joy and glory that it becomes absolutely impossible to tell the difference between a blessing and a trial.

Chapter Twenty-Two

Moses and the Burning Bush

Hebrews 11:27

By faith he forsook Egypt, not fearing the wrath of the king: for he endured, as seeing Him who is invisible.

The three preceding chapters on Moses have centered on one theme, that of how he regarded his own decision to leave Egypt for his brethren. In the verse above we have virtually a restatement by our writer on the same decision, although this time the writer follows Moses' pilgrimage beyond the crisis of the decision itself. We are told not only that he **"endured"** but also that Moses' faith became a **"seeing."**

When Moses made the decision to visit his brethren, he did not intend to return to Egypt. When he entered the land of Goshen, he was not a tourist or a curiosity seeker; he did not regard this as a temporary visit. It was to have been permanent as far as he was concerned. He knew every risk involved.

Visiting the slaves in the land of Goshen was not the sort of thing that a king's son does. It was not a royal appearance, as when cutting a ribbon or breaking a bottle of champagne or dedicating a monument. When he headed for Goshen, he knew he was never to return to Egypt's luxurious palace.

But those people in Goshen probably did not even know who he was, much less what was on his mind when he arrived. Moses thought he would be endearing himself to the Hebrews when he killed an Egyptian. **"For he supposed his brethren would have understood how that God by his hand would deliver them: but they understood not" (Acts 7:25).** We do not know where Moses spent his first night after he first called at Goshen. But he did not go back to the palace.

The writer of the Epistle to the Hebrews tells us that he had consciously renounced his "good life" and that by faith he **"forsook Egypt, not fearing the wrath of the king."** The fear he experienced when he said, **"Surely this thing is known" (Exod. 2:14),** was the consequence of the murder he had committed. Until then the wrath of Pharaoh meant nothing to him. When Moses **"forsook Egypt"** he did not care what Pharaoh thought about it. It was a calculated decision. It was, therefore, not a decision he made after killing the Egyptian. When he discovered that his murder was widespread news, it certainly ensured that he would never go back to the palace; but his decision to leave preceded the murder.

Thus when the account in Exodus says that Moses **"feared" (Exod. 2:14),** it was the fear that emerged within himself for wrongdoing. When our writer says that Moses forsook Egypt, **"not fearing"** the king's wrath, it was the peace that emerged from faith. **"If ye be reproached for the name of Christ, happy are ye...but let none of you suffer as a murderer, or as a thief or as an evildoer, or as a busybody in other men's matters" (I Pet. 4:14-15).**

It is a warning to all lest anyone think, even though he is God's servant—indeed, choice servant—that he is exempt from wrongdoing or that he has a kind of indemnity because of who he is. Some people get very self-righteous when they have acted in faith, and then tend to become careless in other matters. Perhaps even Moses was feeling good about himself for his heroic and godly act in renouncing his Egyptian security. The lesson emerges: *No child of God has indemnity for his sin.*

Moses was to learn one of the most painful truths to be known about God—that God is no respecter of persons. Moses was God's chosen servant; he was raised up for the deliverance of Israel. But Moses was to suffer for this awful deed. This man Moses—God's own selection for Israel's emancipation—was suddenly a man without a country. This man whom God would use to change the face of human history was to be chastised. And yet God's chastening is God's preparation. It is not God "getting even." **"He hath not dealt with us after our sins" (Psa. 103:10).**

God *got even* when on His Son there was laid the iniquity of us all (Isa. 53:6). At the same time, one must face the fact that God deals with us with personal and immediate dignity. Although sin may be atoned for, we often, nonetheless, suffer grievously for the same sin—Moses did—Jonah did—David did. Who among us has not?

Seeing the Invisible

Our writer now pays faith its highest compliment: **"for he endured, as seeing Him who is invisible."** Had Moses been motivated by a spurious faith or a natural motivation, two things would certainly be true: he would never have been chastened (Heb. 12:6), and he would have abandoned his purpose. But he was dealt with. And he **"endured."** At this point our writer seems to contradict what he has previously said about faith. Having said that faith is **"the evidence of things not seen" (Heb. 11:1),** he tells us that Moses endured, **"as seeing Him who is invisible" (Heb. 11:27).** How can this be?

We now come to one of the most sublime but curious events in biblical history. It is one of those events for which there is no natural explanation. There also was no precedent, nor was it repeated again. The episode climaxed forty years of preparation, preceding an era in which Moses would become the greatest leader of men the world would ever know.

It was an incident that coalesced with the secret will of God for His suffering people. **"And it came to pass in process of time, that the king of Egypt died: and the children of Israel sighed by reason of the bondage, and they cried, and their cry came up unto God by reason of the bondage. And God heard their groaning, and God remembered his covenant with Abraham, with Isaac, and with Jacob" (Exod. 2:23-24).** The event that followed was Moses' visit to the burning bush.

The day began like any other day. Moses was tending the flock of his father-in-law Jethro. He gradually led the flock to the back of the desert (perhaps he had been there a thousand times). He came to a mountain, Mount Horeb. We are not told how far up the mountain it was or if it was at the base of the mountain, but Moses happened to notice a bush on fire. Though there may not have been anything particularly unusual about a bush being on fire, Moses kept watching it.

There seemed to be nothing unusual about the fire, but there was something very unusual indeed about the bush—it did not change in substance although it had been on fire for some time. It continued to burn. The bush remained unscathed as though not the first spark had come near it. Curiosity got the best of Moses, and he decided to get to the bottom of this strange sight. **"I will now turn aside, and see this great sight, why the bush is not burnt"** (Exod. 3:3).

What seemed at first to be a phenomenon entirely on the natural level was suddenly transformed by a voice. That voice called out from within the bush, even calling this inquiring man by name. **"And when the Lord saw that he turned aside to see, God called unto him out of the midst of the bush, and said, "Moses, Moses"** (Exod. 3:4). The voice gave Moses explicit advice. **"Draw not nigh hither: put off thy shoes from off thy feet, for the place whereon thou standest is holy ground"** (Exod. 3:5).

At this point the speaker identified Himself: **"I am the God of thy father, the God of Abraham, the God of Isaac, and the God of Jacob"** (Exod. 3:6). We are told that Moses **"hid his face: for he was afraid to look upon God"** (Exod. 3:6).

The man who had endured for forty years was now to experience faith turning to a reality so vivid that our writer claims it was like **"seeing Him who is invisible."** For it did not require faith to see what Moses saw. It was so real that there was no need for faith at the time. It was phenomenal—visible. Moses' faith was temporarily replaced, as it were, by what could literally be seen by his naked eye. No faith was needed to see the burning bush.

This event followed forty years of preparation and preceded forty years of extraordinary ministry. The burning bush was an earnest of the **"recompense of reward"** and also a seeing of the glory of God that was so real Moses could never forget it. And yet, it seems to me, the burning bush prefigured what many of God's people have experienced in their Christian lives, indeed, *after* their initial conversion.

Apart from the historical reality of the burning bush, I regard this event as a kind of symbol that stands for the grace available to those who are awaiting some special ministry after having believed, renounced the world, suffered and endured. Whatever else the burning bush was, it was God's own seal on the life and ministry of Moses. It was God's way of giving Moses the divine approval. The approval was so explicit and objective that Moses could see this phenomenon. After all, a seal is something one can see. What makes a seal a seal? It bears the authentic mark of the Sealer and is inseparably attached to the one sealed.

"Moses, Moses." God identified Himself with Moses. It was, then, an earnest of the recompense of reward. Forty years before Moses had settled, not for the immediate gratification of the natural senses, but for God's promissory note. God now manifested Himself with an immediate taste and sight of that which was to come.

The "Earnest" of the Spirit

When God gives the **"earnest" (see II Cor. 1:22),** it is more than just His Word. It is an expression so real that one is tempted to call it tangible. Faith, for a while, seems redundant. This too was a kind of preparation. Moses needed his preparation in Egypt. He was **"learned in all the wisdom of the Egyptians" (Acts 7:22).** Some think this is the only kind of preparation that is needed—or that matters. Moses was prepared intellectually, but that wasn't enough (even though Moses may have thought so for a while). Moses needed preparation of another kind—suffering. In his case it took forty years. But the time came when he needed yet another important ingredient of his preparation: an undeniable confirmation, something he could never doubt. This was the stage of preparation that empowered him.

The disciples needed the same thing. **"But ye shall receive power, after that the Holy Ghost is come upon you" (Acts 1:8).** When Peter spoke on the Day of Pentecost, he had an assurance that was so full that the resurrection of Jesus could not have been more real if Peter himself had witnessed the whole thing from start to finish with his naked eye. When the Spirit of God came down on the disciples, it provided a level of reality so marvelous that it almost seemed to eliminate the need for faith.

That is what the sealing of the Spirit is. It adds nothing to faith in the sense of making anyone more secure for heaven, but it certainly makes him *feel* more secure! Faith assures of heaven; but the sealing of the Spirit provides a level of reality that is like **"seeing Him who is invisible."** It adds nothing to justification or regeneration; for the one on whom this sealing comes is no more regenerated or justified. Neither can this sealing be said to eradicate all traces of "inbred sin" (although for a while one is tempted to think it does). It gives power. Glory. Witness. A sense of God that, I say, temporarily eliminates the need for faith.

D.L. Moody tells about walking on the streets of Brooklyn when the Spirit unexpectedly came down upon him. Moody says the joy and sense of glory was so powerful and overwhelming that he literally asked God to "stop it," for Moody was afraid that he was going to die on the spot. Many of God's saints have told of similar experiences, and many more have had such without telling a soul.

The need for faith, however, returns. The sight of the burning bush gave way to God's word. **"Moses, Moses."** The bush remained the same. So do we. Nothing is consumed in us. While the fire is visible, we may think we are without sin. Yet sooner or later we are reminded of who we really are—sinners saved by grace. The fire simply releases us to be that for which we have been created and prepared.

The burning bush, or its equivalent, often serves two vital purposes: It is both a reward for having endured and also a special preparation for what is around the corner. It need not be confined to God's more eminent servants. I have talked with many lay people, some uneducated, whose experience with God is as real and definite as any I have read about in the better-known biographies of famous saints.

It is like **"seeing."** It tends almost always to diminish. But one can never forget it. That, too, is part of its purpose.

Chapter Twenty-Three

Moses and the Passover

Hebrews 11:28

Through faith he kept the passover, and the sprinkling of blood, lest he that destroyed the firstborn should touch them.

The importance of knowing the Old Testament will bear repetition. One of the common maladies of modern Christians is their lack of familiarity with the Bible in general and the Old Testament in particular. I think it is fair to say that our lack of theological refinement is due in part to our ignorance of the Old Testament.

It is often forgotten that the earliest church did not have the New Testament—only the Old Testament. The church which had such power and understanding did not have the four Gospels, Paul's epistles, or the Epistle to the Hebrews. It was a good many years before a typical congregation even had more than one New Testament book. What then did they have? The Old Testament. They were forced to look for Messianic passages for themselves, but equally important, they read the whole of the Old Testament in the light of the gospel of Jesus Christ.

Obviously, the Jews had a distinct advantage over the Gentiles in this connection. As Paul summed it up, **"What advantage then hath the Jew?...chiefly, because that unto them were committed the oracles of**

God" **(Rom. 3:1).** This meant that they were spoon-fed on the language of Zion, and the stories that are taken for granted in Hebrews 11 were as common as folklore. Thus, Gentiles had a lot of catching up to do. But it is something they had to do nonetheless. And so do we, if we are to be worthy of having been **"grafted in"** to the natural olive tree (see Rom. 11:16-24).

I would challenge the reader to give much time to reading the Old Testament—all of it, again and again. Begin now. It will be surprising how much you can learn and how much further along you will be, even six months from now. You simply cannot fully grasp the New Testament unless you give commensurate time to the Old Testament.

Our writer continues with the great Moses, this time jumping from his personal faith and experience to his wider ministry. Hebrews 11:24-27 deals with his faith and initial preparation period; the two remaining verses pertaining to Moses deal with him as a great leader of men. A lot has happened between the burning bush and the event to which our present verse refers. The burning bush was God's seal on Moses' life and ministry; it was equally the assurance of God's will to deliver the children of Israel from their awful bondage in Egypt. It meant as much to Israel as it did to Moses. So it is with any unusual, authentic experience of God given to a man or woman. It is not merely to provide unquestionable clarity concerning God's love and will, for its ultimate purpose is to bless others.

The Art of Leadership

We might easily have thought that all the preparation Moses needed was over. Surely by now he was ready. But required for the coming deliverance of the children of Israel is still more preparation for Moses (not to mention the people he will try to lead). Why should Moses be given yet more preparation? Because he needed it.

It is a grave warning to all of us who are leaders to remember that we are always learning and always being prepared. If physicians can be involved daily in the "practice" of medicine, how much more should the physician of the soul soberly admit that he is in a *practice of leading* men.

Moses was learning as he went along. We never outgrow the need of more preparation. The highest confirmation of dignity by the Most High God is His bestowal of continued preparation upon those He intends to use. Furthermore, no task before us is ever precisely the same as one which went before.

Moses' post-burning bush and pre-Passover preparation was that of making him a leader of men. His training was more painful and rigorous after the burning bush than any he had undergone before. It was his post-burning bush and pre-Passover experience that made him a great leader. This is what produces greatness—God's sovereign dealing with a man. It is what is missing today. Whatever else this generation has witnessed, it is surely this: a dearth of greatness.

Look at nations today! On both sides of the Atlantic there has been a scrambling for power by little men; it is a pitiful, melancholy sight. The difference between a great man and a small man is this: A great man is ambitious for principle; a little man is ambitious for position. When a man is truly ambitious for a valid principle, the position will seek him. Moses was a truly great man and an extraordinary leader of men. Most "leaders" of today's generation are followers. They take a straw vote, find out where fifty-one per cent of the people stand, then loudly announce their "strong" stand as though it was their own. Today's "leader" wets his finger, holds it up to the wind, and then doggedly leaps a step or two ahead of the trend, claiming to be leading it. It is an ominous sign of the times when God is not preparing men for true leadership.

The most painful lesson Moses had to learn as a leader was that people are seldom guided by an underlying principle—they are guided by favorable results. As long as things were going well, Moses was highly exalted among the children of Israel. But any sort of setback made them as angry as they had been happy. One day they were carrying Moses on their shoulders; the next day they were cursing him. When Moses first announced to Israel that God had sent him and Aaron to lead them, and when they had performed **"signs"** before them, **"the people believed...they bowed their heads and worshiped"** (Exod. 4:30-31).

But when Pharaoh did not respond to Moses' initial command to let the people leave Egypt, they confronted Moses and shouted: **"The Lord**

look upon you, and judge; because ye have made our savour to be abhorred in the eyes of Pharaoh, and in the eyes of his servants, to put a sword in their hand to slay us" (Exod. 5:21). This kind of murmuring would be repeated by the children of Israel many times in the next few years.

A more subtle kind of preparation for Moses was this: His problems, rather than being personal ones, became those of the kingdom of God. Some of us never make this transition. Some of us are preoccupied with our personal, family problems all our lives; though our concern for the kingdom of God ought to be primary, it isn't. The difference between a typical Christian today and a man of God can be discovered by whether he lives for personal security and pleasure or by a transcending concern for the kingdom of God.

Moses was a family man; he was a husband and a father. There were family concerns (see Exod. 4:18-26). But the time came when his chief problems were not personal ones but those that pertained to the kingdom of God. What was once a concern for personal survival had become a concern for the survival of God's people. This was the new Moses—not merely the one who had refused to be called Pharaoh's grandson, but the Moses that would confront Pharaoh in order to deliver Israel.

When our writer tells us that Moses kept the Passover, we must not forget the pre-Passover details of Moses' life. The Passover was also preceded by a number of fruitless encounters with Pharaoh. The truest words Pharaoh ever uttered were these: **"I know not the Lord" (Exod. 5:2).** But Pharaoh was destined to know Him—in a most alarming manner. There followed a series of plagues upon Egypt. At first when Moses warned of a coming plague, Pharaoh thought he was bluffing. But Pharaoh soon learned that Moses was not.

There came a series of plagues, and each succeeding plague became more destructive: blood (Exod. 7:19), frogs (8:2), lice (8:16), flies (8:21), destruction of cattle (9:3), boils (9:9), hail and fire (9:22), locusts (10:12) and darkness (10:21). These nine plagues began with Pharaoh's magicians duplicating the phenomena but, along the way, they became completely baffled and defeated and were unable to keep up with what God was doing. It shows that Satan can go a rather long way in counterfeiting some of the authentic things God can do in the church.

As these plagues continued, we read again and again: God hardened Pharaoh's heart (Exod. 7:3, 22; 8:15, 19, 32; 9:7, 12, 35; 10:20, 27). **"For the scripture saith unto Pharaoh, Even for this same purpose have I raised thee up, that I might shew my power in thee, and that my name might be declared throughout all the earth. Therefore hath he mercy on whom he will have mercy, and whom he will he hardeneth" (Rom. 9:17-18).**

We might wish to ask: "Why didn't God make any of these nine plagues conclusive in securing Israel's release?" (For He could have.) I suspect the answer lies partly in this: God wanted to make sure that the children of Israel would never forget the pit from which they were dug. Men can be so forgetful. To the extent we forget, we become ungrateful. God also wanted to show His power in Egypt, that heathen men might know the true God (see Exod. 11:9). But the ultimate answer to this question is surely this: The Passover was to prefigure the greatest redemptive event in all human history—the atoning death of Jesus Christ on the cross.

Moses, the greatest leader of men the world has ever known, faced his greatest test yet. After nine, horrendous plagues, Pharaoh remained adamant. The children of Israel were waiting in the wings—wondering, doubting, and not a little discouraged. No plague had succeeded. Would anything change Pharaoh's mind? This surely was the question of questions.

Our writer, therefore, tells us that **"through faith"** Moses kept the Passover. It was Moses' task to face the children of Israel with a most unusual, if not irrational, request. Nothing like this had ever been done before; it was utterly unprecedented. The nearest we can come to a precedent is the sacrifice of Abel (see chapter 4), but what Moses was prescribing for the children of Israel was without any historical precedent:

> **In the tenth day of this month they shall take to them every man a lamb, according to the house of their fathers, a lamb for an house...without blemish, a male of the first year...keep it up until the fourteenth day of the same month: and the whole assembly of the congregation of Israel shall kill it in the evening. And they shall take of the blood, and strike it on the two side posts and on the upper door post of the houses, wherein they shall eat it...For I will**

pass through the land of Egypt this night, and will smite all the firstborn in the land of Egypt, both man and beast; and against all the gods of Egypt I will execute judgment: I am the Lord. And the blood shall be to you for a token upon the houses where ye are: and when I see the blood, I will *pass over* you, and the plague shall not be upon you to destroy you, when I smite the land of Egypt" (Exod. 12:3-13).

Following God's Instructions

That was the command from God to Moses, and it was Moses' job to get the children of Israel to obey it. Not only was this without precedent, there was no rational basis for thinking it would work! There was not the slightest reason for thinking that a sprinkling of a little blood from a lamb would make any difference at all. It was therefore Moses' task to persuade the children of Israel to follow his orders and to do so in every detail.

"Through faith he kept the passover, and the sprinkling of the blood" (Heb. 11:28). It was an act of faith. When our writer tells us that Moses kept the Passover, it means that Moses believed that God was serious in His promise to destroy every firstborn living in Egypt—both man and beast. Moses believed that God would literally do that—even destroying the children of Israel's firstborn—if they were not protected by the sprinkling of blood. It was Moses' affirmation of God's word, but also of His wrath.

Moses believed God. He therefore called all the elders of Israel and gave them the above instructions. **"For the Lord will pass through to smite the Egyptians; and when he seeth the blood upon the lintel, and on the two side posts, the Lord will *pass over* the door, and will not suffer the destroyer to come in unto your houses to smite you" (Exod. 12:23).**

There was no reason to believe this would work. But Moses followed the Lord's instructions carefully. And the people? **"The people bowed the head and worshipped"** and **"did as the Lord had commanded Moses and Aaron" (Exod. 12:27-28).** Moses had succeeded in getting the people to follow through. Every house in Israel that evening had the sight of sprinkled blood on their door posts.

What a sight! What would any Egyptian have thought if he had happened to walk through the land of Goshen that evening? An Egyptian would have known that the children of Israel were up to something, but there was no way of knowing *what*—nor would it have been believed if told. For the simplicity of obeying God is always **"foolishness"** to the natural man (I Cor. 2:14).

The sun set in the east as on any other day. Families gathered in their various homes, probably seated around tables. The lambs had been roasted in fire. The food was not a gourmet's delight or characterized by the sort of relaxation one prefers at mealtime. The lamb was to be eaten **"in haste"** ("trepidation" is a better translation) with unleavened bread and bitter herbs (Exod. 12:8, 11). It was now getting dark. Perhaps hearts were beating faster. Children, who could not understand what was going on, were tempted to go to the door and take a peek outside. Hours passed. It seemed unusually quiet in Goshen. Perhaps Moses had miscalculated? How does one know anybody is really being destroyed and that one is truly being spared?

All was quiet in Goshen but **"there was a great cry in Egypt; for there was not a house where there was not one dead"** (Exod. 12:30). For at **"midnight the Lord smote all the firstborn in the land of Egypt, from the firstborn of Pharaoh that sat on his throne unto the firstborn of the captive that was in the dungeon; and all the firstborn of cattle"** (Exod. 12:29). As the Passover prefigures the atoning death of Jesus, so also does the destroyer in the land of Egypt prefigure the eternal destruction of the wicked. We who have **"peace with God through our Lord Jesus Christ"** (Rom. 5:1) cannot bear the wailing and gnashing of teeth of the impenitent. But our not hearing them is no sign they are not being dealt with. It is our duty to look to Jesus and be thankful we have been **"saved from wrath through Him"** (Rom. 5:9).

Those who were spared on the night of the Passover owed their salvation to the sprinkling of blood. By faith Moses kept the Passover **"and the sprinkling of blood, lest he that destroyed the firstborn should touch them"** (Heb. 11:28). There is a widespread view that the literal shedding of blood does not matter, that it is merely the *death* of Jesus that saves us. But if that were true, the children of Israel could have been content with the eating of the roasted lamb and bitter herbs; surely the destroyer could see inside the homes as well as outside.

But no, God says, **"When I see the *blood*, I will pass over you"** (Exod. 12:13). **"Much more then, being now justified by His blood, we shall be saved from wrath through Him"** (Rom. 5:9). The four living creatures and twenty-four elders sang a new song: "**Thou art worthy to take the book, and to open the seals thereof: for thou wast slain, and hast redeemed us to God *by thy blood*"** (Rev. 5:9).

When I was a boy we used to sing:

Christ our Redeemer died on the cross,
Died for the sinner, paid all his due;
Sprinkle your soul with the blood of the Lamb,
And I will pass, will pass over you.

It makes no sense. But it's God's word. Moses took it seriously. All Israel was glad he did.

Chapter Twenty-Four

MOSES AND CROSSING THE RED SEA

Hebrews 11:29

By faith they passed through the Red Sea as by dry land: which the Egyptians assaying to do were drowned.

One of the more interesting questions regarding Moses and the Book of Exodus is this: Which is the greater event, the Passover or the crossing of the Red Sea? The Passover was the event that finally persuaded Pharaoh to let Israel go; the crossing of the Red Sea is perhaps the most spectacular miracle in the Old Testament. It also ended all encounters with Pharaoh.

Trying to figure out such a question is like debating whether our Lord's crucifixion or His resurrection was the more important event. The only answer is the ultimate answer: They absolutely go together and cannot be separated.

The above verse brings us to our final study of Moses. We have followed the writer of the Epistle to the Hebrews, tracing Moses' life from his birth to his conversion, from his preparation to the Passover. The Passover was the straw that broke the camel's back where Pharaoh was concerned. The nine plagues prior to the Passover failed to move Pharaoh's heart. But the Passover achieved its end. The destruction of all the firstborn in Egypt, including Pharaoh's own son, resulted in Pharaoh's finally letting the children of Israel go. **"And he called for Moses and Aaron by night, and said, Rise up, and get you forth from among my people, both ye and the children of Israel; and go, serve the Lord, as ye have said"** (Exod. **12:31**).

We are told that **"the children of Israel went out with an high hand"** (**Exod. 14:8**—**"marching out boldly"** NIV). They took from the Egyptians **"jewels of silver, and jewels of gold, and raiment: and the Lord gave the people favor in the sight of the Egyptians, so that they lent unto them such things as they required. And they spoiled the Egyptians"** (Exod. **12:35-36**).

Exodus 13:17 is a most significant verse in the life of the children of Israel subsequent to their departure from Egypt. **"When Pharaoh had let the people go, that God led them not through the land of the Philistines, although that was near; for God said, Lest peradventure the people repent when they see war, and they return to Egypt."** In other words, there was (geographically speaking) a direct route to Canaan. It would have got them there sooner; it would have avoided that fatal pocket in which they got trapped at the Red Sea. But God knew best.

There is no hint, however, that the children of Israel knew at the time that they were being led this way; Moses, writing the history, tells us this. It is an illustration of the fact that God deals with us according to our mentality, frame of mind, and depth of strength; He knows us better than we know ourselves. And yet we may ask: "Why did God permit this?" Exodus 13:17 gives an insightful hint: It was the least of the evil options set before them. Most of us are like Peter, who imagined himself stronger against temptation than he really was (John 13:37).

Wherever He may guide me, no want shall turn me back;

My Shepherd is beside me, and nothing can I lack:

His wisdom ever waketh, His sight is never dim;

He knows the way He taketh, and I will walk with Him.

Led by a Cloud

But how were the children of Israel led, and how certain was this guidance? The answer is by one of the strangest phenomena in the Old Testament. **"And the Lord went before them by day in a pillar of a cloud, to lead them the way; and by night in a pillar of fire, to give them light; to go by day and night: He took not away the pillar of the cloud by day, nor the pillar of fire by night, from before the people" (Exodus 13:21-22).** As Calvin put it, "It was a marvelous act of loving kindness that, accommodating Himself to their ignorance, God familiarly presented Himself before their eyes."

Two things may be said about this demonstration of the glory of God. The pillar of cloud and fire was (1) unprecedented and (2) objective (that is, visible). God delights in doing new things—sufficiently different from what He has done before that we may be tested to see whether we are following Him alone, or tradition.

We all need to learn the lesson of historical precedence without being controlled by it. Had there been a closed mind to any new way of being led—that is, open only to what they had already seen, Moses would have rejected this phenomenon. But he knew it was God's gracious guidance. The pillar of cloud and fire was an objective witness to God's affirmation of Israel. It was not unlike the burning bush in that faith was not required to see it. In a sense, it prefigured what many would now call revival—not merely a week of services but an unmistakable demonstration of God's power.

However, the same phenomenon of glory can have the opposite effect upon another group, compared to the effect it has upon those it gives great comfort. It was undoubted guidance and consolation for Israel; it was the ground of confusion and frustration for Egypt (as we shall see). Let no one think, therefore, that a great revival (oh, may it come) will produce the same universal and uniform effect. It intensifies and magnifies the love of God in some, and intensifies and magnifies hostility towards the same God in others.

The story of the departure of the children of Israel is a remarkable display of the stubbornness of the human heart in nearly all concerned. First, in Pharaoh. He was given now exactly ten irrefutable demonstrations of God's power and wrath against Egypt. It was not until the death of his own firstborn that he gave in. But, amazingly, he came to himself and changed his mind about letting Israel go.

Like a drunk becoming sober—or an unchanged heart making a profession of faith ("Why did I do that?"), Pharaoh exclaimed, **"Why have we done this, that we have let Israel go from serving us?"** (Exod. 14:5). Consequently Pharaoh **"made ready his chariot"** and **"took six hundred chosen chariots, and all the chariots of Egypt, and captains over every one of them"** (Exod. 14:6-7).

Such recalcitrance, however, was not limited to Pharaoh. The children of Israel soon had their first test. Question: Would they affirm the God of their deliverance and would they pass their first test? Answer: They did not. Pharaoh began chasing after the children of Israel and the latter saw the Egyptians coming. **"They were sore afraid: and the children of Israel cried out unto the Lord"** (Exod. 14:10).

Their reaction was perhaps quite normal and natural, but they did not leave it at that. **"And they said unto Moses, Because there were no graves in Egypt hast thou taken us away to die in the wilderness? wherefore hast thou dealt with us, to carry us forth out of Egypt?...For it had been better for us to serve the Egyptians, than that we should die in the wilderness"** (Exod. 14:11-12). It is unthinkable that such people could be so forgetful and unthankful.

A weakness can be seen in Moses as well. It is wonderful that the Bible lets us see the great men as they really were. In an odd sort of way, I can sometimes get almost as much strength from seeing the weakness of a great man as I can his strength. For it makes me feel that God can use even me!

Moses' first reaction (his public face) to Israel's murmuring was this: **"Fear ye not, stand still, and see the salvation of the Lord, which he will shew to you today: for the Egyptians whom ye have seen today, ye shall see them again no more for ever. The Lord shall fight for you, and ye shall hold your peace"** (Exod. 14:13-14). And that was a wonderful word. Moses meant it. And it was true.

But hidden between the lines in the very next verse there is to be seen Moses' heart of hearts. Moses himself might have inserted a verse between Exodus 14:14 and Exodus 14:15. It is the most significant non-verse I have yet come across. Had there been a verse inserted between verse 14 and verse 15, I suspect it would have read, "And Moses himself cried unto the Lord." And yet verse 15 virtually puts that very verse there, for we read: **"And the Lord said unto Moses, Wherefore criest thou unto me?"** (**"Why are you crying out to me?"** NIV).

What had happened was this. Moses had boldly stated, **"Stand still, and see the salvation of the Lord."** But Moses seems to have begun to reflect most soberly upon what he had just said. He became frightened by his own words. He himself began crying to the Lord! After making that bold pronouncement to the people, Moses saw out of the corner of his eye Pharaoh coming with his chariots. He had told Israel to **"stand still."** He now thinks: "What have I done?" He cries to God: "O God, what have I done?"

However, God said to Moses, **"Why are you crying out to me?"** For there comes a time when we should quit praying and start doing. There is a time when prayer is a cowardly thing to do; it is often the biggest cop-out in the world. Some people opt for the sacrifice of more praying rather than obey what God has already told them to do. God said to Moses, "Get off your knees." **"Wherefore criest thou unto me? speak unto the children of Israel, that they go forward: But lift thou up thy rod, and stretch out thine hand over the sea, and divide it: and the children of Israel shall go on dry ground through the midst of the sea"** (Exod. 14:15-16).

"Quit your crying, Moses," the Lord told him. **"LIFT UP YOUR ROD"!** And he did.

The Lord will not ask us to do what He will not also enable us to do. **"And Moses stretched out his hand over the sea; and the Lord caused the sea to go back by a strong east wind all that night, and made the sea dry land, and the waters were divided"** (Exod. 14:21).

"By faith they passed through the Red Sea as by dry land." Who can deny that God could have divided the sea without Moses' rod? God can do anything. Boys and girls, God *could* do your homework for you. God *could* save men apart from preaching. God could strike every man down as he did Saul of Tarsus on the road to Damascus. But God gave Moses a rod, and He wanted him to use it. God forced Moses to initiate, as it were, this spectacular miracle—by obedience.

WHEN YOUR OPTIONS ARE DOWN TO ONE

Moses didn't really have any other choice. God has a way of bringing our options down to one. God has a way of securing the response to His word that He wants. God did not lead the children of Israel through the land of the Philistines, lest they turn back altogether. He wanted instead to bring them to the place where they would have no choice but to turn utterly to Him. That was "the crunch"—no turning back.

There was nothing to do but to lift up that rod—and watch God do the rest. He may have thought, "I've never done this before. I may look like a fool. But here goes!" Up the rod came. Across the wind came. God did the rest. By the way, that was not wind at the level of the Spirit as at Pentecost when God sent a **"rushing mighty wind"** (Acts 2:2). This was wind, wind at the level of nature—**"a strong east wind"**—wind that obeyed the summons of its Sovereign Creator.

They walked across. They didn't swim. They walked. They didn't run. They walked. They enjoyed this spectacular sight up close. Some were given the honor of carrying the bones of Joseph. They had pockets full of loot, jewels, valuables. Parents kept moving their children along. There was no need to say, "Don't forget to wear your galoshes." It was dry ground.

Parents could say to their children, "Take a close look at this. This is our God at work. Don't ever forget it." There was no need to watch for puddles. As long as nobody was allergic to dust, there was no problem. By faith they passed through the Red Sea **"as by dry land."** They went across the midst of the sea **"upon dry ground: and the waters were a wall unto them on their right hand, and on their left"** (Exod. 14:22).

Pharaoh, in the meantime, made the most unwise calculation to be seen among the Egyptians yet. It was one of the most foolish mistakes in military history. What was it? The Egyptians thought that they could do what the children of Israel had done. Our verse continues: **"which the Egyptians assaying to do were drowned"** (**"but when the Egyptians tried to do so, they were drowned"** NIV). **"And the Egyptians pursued, and went in after them to the midst of the sea, even all Pharaoh's horses, his chariots, and his horsemen."**

The Egyptians' magicians were able to do some things that Moses and Aaron had done—but only up to a point. Their most fatal error was trying to continue the pursuit of Israel across the Red Sea. But they realized their folly too late. For the same pillar of fire and cloud that had been Israel's guidance became Egypt's confusion.

In the morning watch the Lord looked down from the pillar of fire and cloud at the Egyptian army and threw it into confusion. He made the wheels of their chariots swerve so that they had difficulty driving. And the Egyptians said, **"Let's get away from the Israelites! The Lord is fighting for them against Egypt" (Exod. 14:24-25 NIV).** God had once more **"hardened"** Egypt (Exod. 14:4). The same hardening that temporarily blocked the hopes of Israel finally brought the ultimate downfall of her enemies.

When God hardens a man, it will always end for His glory. God's hardening Pharaoh is simply one way of describing the activity of the devil. Satan can work only when he has ground to do so. Pharaoh's hardening gave the devil ground. But, as always, Satan went too far in the end—and he lost.

Moses' work at the Red Sea was not quite finished. Equally great and glorious was Moses' final use of that rod. The equally great miracle was the way the same waters ended the Egyptians' threat. **"And the waters returned, and covered the chariots, and the horsemen, and all the host of Pharaoh that came into the sea after them; there remained not so much as one of them" (Exod. 14:28).**

The rod that was used to deliver Israel was used to condemn the Egyptians. The same Word that saves some will condemn others. The same blood which saves some will condemn others. As Abel's blood cried up from the ground, so the blood of Jesus remains **"no more sacrifice for**

sins" to those who reject Him, but rather brings **"a certain fearful looking for of judgment"** (**Heb. 10:26-27**).

Faith does what cannot be done by those who do not believe. And yet, (perhaps our most important lesson from this story) faith also does what crying to God cannot do. There comes a time that we must act, do, obey. Lift up your rod. If that is what God has told you to do, nothing else will happen until you do it. Doing it is faith.

Chapter Twenty-Five

The Walls of Jericho

Hebrews 11:30

By faith the walls of Jericho fell down, after they were compassed about seven days.

Our study moves from Moses to Joshua. It is interesting that Joshua himself is not named in the above verse although he was the central figure behind the event that is described by our writer. Joshua was Moses' successor. He and Caleb were the only two living souls of the "Passover generation" who were permitted to enter the Promised Land—the land of Canaan. Of the others God said, **"I was grieved with that generation, and said, They do always err in their heart; and they have not known my ways. So I sware in my wrath, They shall not enter into my rest" (Heb. 3:10-11).**

Long before, Moses had sent a group of men to investigate the land of Canaan. Caleb was one of those, and he insisted that the time was ripe for conquering that land: **"Let us go up at once, and possess it; for we are well able to overcome it" (Num. 13:30).** But Caleb was outnumbered: **"We be not able to go up against the people; for they are stronger than we" (Num. 13:31).** The result was that the entry into Canaan was postponed for many years. Only Joshua and Caleb survived that generation.

One of the sadder events in the life of Moses was the disclosure that he too would be deprived of entering Canaan. It is very sad indeed that the very man whom God had sent to deliver Israel from Pharaoh and who patiently led a rebellious people through the wilderness for forty years should himself be told that he would not be granted entrance to Canaan. But Moses had become too personally involved on the occasion when he smote the rock instead of only speaking to it (when water was so desperately needed). The sin was so grievous to God that Moses was at once told: **"Because ye believed me not, to sanctify me in the eyes of the children of Israel, therefore ye shall not bring this congregation into the land"** (Num. 20:12).

This event shows that the greatest of saints have a vestige of carnal pride remaining in them, and however intimately they may have been dealt with by God, they never have a "claim" upon God. God remains no respecter of persons. Moses' consolation was that he was given opportunity to survey the land from atop Mount Nebo. That was the nearest he got to Canaan.

"Moses my servant is dead; now therefore arise, go over this Jordan, thou, and all this people, unto the land which I do give to them, even to the children of Israel" (Josh. 1:2). This was God's word to Joshua. The time had come. At long last the prophecy of Joseph was about to be fulfilled. But it was an entirely new generation, one that had not seen the mighty acts of God back in Egypt. God had started all over again, and now a people had been prepared. They affirmed their loyalty to God and to His servant Joshua: **"All that thou commandest us we will do, and whithersoever thou sendest us, we will go"** (Josh. 1:16).

Our verse (Hebrews 11:30) tells what happened shortly *after* they crossed the Jordan River into Canaan. But one cannot help but notice in the meantime that our writer has jumped from the crossing of the Red Sea to the fall of Jericho, passing over events that took place in the preceding forty years—not the least of which was the giving of the Ten Commandments on Mount Sinai. We might also ask, why not deal with the actual entry into Canaan itself? Was not this the event that had been looked forward to for so many, many years? Why then should our writer pass over these events in this faith chapter?

Things the "Faith Chapter" Left Out

I believe that the reason our writer did not deal with the events of Mount Sinai is precisely because Hebrews 11 is indeed a "faith" chapter. Whatever else can be said about the law, we must take most seriously Paul's word: **"The law is not of faith"** (Gal. 3:12). The NIV has it: **"The law is not based on faith."** Indeed, Paul asked: **"Wherefore then serveth the law?** *It was added* **because of transgressions"** (Gal. 3:19). The Law was never God's ultimate purpose for His people in the first place. It is a great pity that the Law was ever made necessary—but it was **"because of transgressions."** The writer of the epistle to the Hebrews has the same theology and treats the event in this chapter with a benign neglect.

The reason for the omission of the crossing of the Jordan into Canaan is equally easy to see, if only because of our writer's thesis in Hebrews 11:10-17. For the land of Canaan was never meant to be the ultimate destination for the children of Israel. **"He hath prepared for them a city"** (Heb. 11:16). Canaan, then, was no more permanent by Joshua's time than it had been for Abraham. It is the tragedy of Israel, both then and now, that *physical land* became the ultimate thing for them. Our writer does not even mention their crossing the Jordan.

Indeed, the entry of the children of Israel into the land of Canaan is the great anticlimax of the Old Testament. When one considers how eagerly this moment had been anticipated; how memorable were the events of the Passover and the crossing of the Red Sea; that the very people who yearned for it most were deprived of it, and that those who did cross the Jordan were a truly obedient people; it is rather surprising that more is not made of it—even in the Old Testament! For it had been forecast as a land of **"rest,"** but once they got there it was anything but rest. **"About forty thousand prepared for war passed over before the Lord unto battle, to the plains of Jericho"** (Josh. 4:13).

Our writer to the Hebrews plainly states: **"If Jesus (which should read "Joshua") had given them rest, then would he not afterward have spoken of another day"** (Heb. 4:8). Our writer knew what the Jews generally never understood: the Promised Land was really given to Israel in a **"figure."** This is the way Abraham got Isaac back; the same happened to

Isaac and again to Jacob. This idea of **"figure"** or **"shadow"** is one of the keys to understanding the entire epistle to the Hebrews.

The land of Canaan, according to our writer, was a type of the full assurance promised to those who believe (see Heb. 4:10). But from a human perspective, Canaan was anything but rest. Indeed, for the next several hundred years this land would see enough blood shed to fill a thousand seas.

What our writer does, then, is to seize upon the first opportunity that demonstrates naked faith after they entered Canaan—the siege of Jericho. Although the inheritance of Canaan is to be grasped ultimately at the level of the Spirit, we must not underestimate the fact that God was with Joshua and the children of Israel in a most powerful way. God did, in fact, promise the land of Canaan to Abraham, Isaac and Jacob—and Joseph. Not only that, God was going to do wonderful things for them as undeniable confirmations of His guidance.

God ordered them to destroy Jericho. That was to be their first test. It was no use moving deeper into Canaan with an unconquered foe behind them. It would be folly to postpone this confrontation. One must learn this in the Christian life. There is no place for sweeping the dirt under the carpet in the kingdom of God. If God convicts us of a certain duty, it will not go away. We must do it now or suffer for postponing it.

But Joshua and all the children of Israel ran into a problem—a real problem: Jericho was shut up. It was tighter than a drum. Israel's reputation had preceded them, and the people of Jericho, knowing that they would be attacked, had sealed themselves inside the walled city. There was no physical way to conquer this city of Jericho.

When God's Advice Seems Like Nonsense

There is now to be seen the most curious, if not ridiculous, advice God ever gave to intelligent people.

> **Ye shall compass the city, all ye men of war, and go round about the city once. Thus shalt thou do six days. And seven priests shall bear before the ark seven trumpets of rams' horns: and the seventh day ye shall compass the city seven times and the priests shall blow**

with the trumpets. And it shall come to pass, that when they make a long blast with the ram's horn, and when ye hear the sound of the trumpet, all the people shall shout with a great shout; and the wall of the city shall fall down flat, and the people shall ascend up every man straight before him (Josh. 6:3-5).

By any man's judgment this advice must be regarded as sheer nonsense. And so it is—unless that is what God tells you to do. If God tells you to do it, following it is the highest wisdom.

But why should God give advice like this? Why bother to compass a walled city they could never penetrate? Why do it once a day—for seven days? Why blow trumpets? Why all this seven times on the seventh day? Answer: God puts us through ridiculous tests to see whether our faith will persevere. God tests our obedience by strange trials. **"Think it not strange concerning the fiery trial which is to try you, as though some strange thing happened unto you" (I Pet. 4:12).**

God sometimes tests our love by putting us through irrational, disjointed and unconnected series of odd occurrences. God puts unprecedented counsel and guidance to us lest we derive strength from the past rather than the present. God also puts us through trials never to be repeated lest we keep looking for the same kind of word—or victory.

There was nothing magical in the number seven or in the blowing of trumpets. Had they tried this again, they would have been laughed out of existence. But that was what they were to do then, and nothing else would have worked. God could have done it differently, yes. God *could* have sent an angel directly to Jericho to blow it up—without faith. And God *could* have parted the Red Sea without Moses' rod. But when God is truly with us to give an irrefutable confirmation of His approval and power, it is likely that such will be preceded by orders sufficiently different from any other we have had or known about. God shows His glory only when there can be no natural explanation for it.

Joshua gave explicit orders: **"Ye shall not shout, nor make any noise with your voice, neither shall any word proceed out of your mouth, until the day I bid you shout; then shall ye shout (Josh. 6:10).** This command was given to ensure that there were no slip-ups, no accidents or chance happenings to rival God's actual work. But it was also given in order that nothing could share the spotlight with faith. For if there was any other cause for the walls of Jericho to fall, faith could not get the credit.

Quietly and carefully the children of Israel walked around the city on the first day. The only sound was the blowing of trumpets. They returned to the camp and went to bed. They did the same thing on the second day, the third, fourth, fifth and sixth day. On the seventh day they walked around the city as they had done for the previous six days. The only sound was the blowing of trumpets. Nothing happened. But nothing was supposed to happen.

They walked around the city the second time on this seventh day. Nothing happened. They walked around Jericho the third time, the fourth, fifth and sixth time. In the meantime those inside Jericho may have thought that those Israelites walking around outside were a company of fools. They may have chuckled as they heard nothing but the sound of trumpets, thinking to themselves that this was one city that would not be shaken.

But immediately after the children of Israel had walked around the city the seventh time, the priests blew their trumpets and Joshua said to the people, **"SHOUT; FOR THE LORD HATH GIVEN YOU THE CITY" (Josh. 6:16).** When the people shouted, it was a great shout. The consequence? **"The wall fell down flat, so that the people went up into the city, every man straight before him, and they took the city" (Josh. 6:20).**

What destroyed the city? Encompassing it seven times? The blowing of trumpets? Shouting? No. None of these. **"By *faith* the walls of Jericho fell down, after they were compassed about seven days" (Heb. 11:30).** The children of Israel followed Joshua's leadership perfectly. They did not question the apparent absurdity of the command. They simply did what they were told to do. Did it work? Yes, it did.

We are not told how the fall of Jericho came about in terms of natural phenomena. In the case of the crossing of the Red Sea, God sent a wind. Whether in the case of the falling of Jericho's walls it was an earthquake or a tornado or something else does not matter. Ultimately it was the Holy

THE WALLS OF JERICHO

Spirit. **"Not by might, nor by power, but by my Spirit, saith the Lord of hosts" (Zech. 4:6).** Faith did it, nothing else. Our writer does not say "by faith Joshua" or "by faith the people"; he only says **"by faith the walls."** Obviously it was not that the walls had faith; rather, his point is that there was no natural explanation for what happened, and no one could take the credit—only God.

Joshua had led the children of apostate parents to a most wonderful obedience. In a sense this is one of the most encouraging aspects of the story. The second generation is often the end of a line, especially if the first generation had been obedient and owned of God. But in this case the opposite was true; the second generation was the beginning of a line, for the first generation had not known God's ways. It is yet another proof that the continuity of God's people is not dependent upon natural causes or human ability, for God is able to break into any situation.

God loves to defy natural explanations for what He does.

Chapter Twenty-Six

Rahab the Harlot

Hebrews 11:31

By faith the harlot Rahab perished not with them that believed not, when she had received the spies with peace.

Our study of Hebrews 11 now takes an interesting twist. It is not surprising that the great "faith" chapter should include Noah or Enoch; Abraham, Isaac and Jacob; or Moses. Neither is it surprising that a woman should be included among the people of faith; for Sarah was given prominence in verse 11, and Moses' mother was the central figure of verse 23. But that a harlot should be regarded as a person of high stature in this chapter seems at first to be quite incongruous.

Not long before, Moses had given the Ten Commandments, two of which were the forbidding of adultery and the bearing of false witness. Who would ever have thought then that a person who told a bare-faced lie and who was commonly known as a prostitute would be dignified in sacred history? We are not talking about the unfortunate overtaking of a moral, upstanding girl who suddenly falls into sin, or the respectable middle-class woman who carries on a secret affair, and then repents. Rahab was a harlot.

The Bible is full of surprises. Here is a story that ruggedly cuts across the very morality that some think is the highest good. It is an account that demonstrates the way God sometimes seems to break all the rules that we have defended and lived by for years. Whatever else could be said about Israel's first battle in the land of Canaan, none could ever escape the knowledge that, in Israel's pivotal and crucial moment of history in her new land, God used an unpatriotic prostitute to ensure Israel's safety and security.

Not only did Israel exalt her, but early Christians did as well. She is mentioned in Matthew's genealogy (Matt. 1:5). She married into one of Israel's most prominent families and even became a link in the direct bloodline chain of the promised Messiah. James puts her alongside Abraham to illustrate what he means by justification by works (James 2:25).

Before Joshua led the children of Israel across the Jordan, he had dispatched two spies to investigate things in Jericho. The writer to the Hebrews might well have made mention of the two spies, for they were men of courage. But they were to be upstaged by Rahab. When these two spies entered Jericho, they needed a place to stay. They were no doubt spotted by the upstanding, patriotic citizens of Jericho. It was not particularly advantageous to be a foreigner; but to be regarded as a spy for Israel was to be placed in a most dangerous position.

The children of Israel by now had a widespread reputation for one of the worst kinds of colonialism ever known. This reputation was well known in this walled city of Jericho. These spies weren't likely to find Jerichoites the friendliest people in the world. So where would the spies find lodging? Answer: they eventually called on the town prostitute—and were given a place to stay. Nobody else would have them.

For our writer tells us that the other people of Jericho were given opportunity to befriend the spies. Our verse reads: **"Rahab perished not with them that believed not."** Israel's reputation was not known by Rahab only; she says so. **"All the inhabitants of the land faint because of you,"** she said to the spies, **"for we have heard how the Lord dried up the water of the Red Sea for you, when ye came out of Egypt; and what ye did unto the two kings of the Amorites"** (Josh. 2:9-10).

Lying for the Glory of God?

The very knowledge that made the citizens of Jericho hostile to the spies is what made Rahab anxious to befriend them. What made the citizens of Jericho absolutely certain that they should reject the spies is precisely what made Rahab absolutely certain she should **"receive them with peace."** Such a response to the spies set a pattern for the gospel. The same gospel that hardens some softens others. It is no wonder, then, that our writer tells us that Rahab did what she did **"by faith."**

The word passed on to the king of Jericho that Rahab had let the two spies into her home. We may ask: Why didn't the king look at the children of Israel like Rahab did? He could have given the two spies the key to the city. Paul answers this kind of question: **"Ye see your calling, brethren, how that not many wise men after the flesh, not many mighty, not many noble, are called: but God hath chosen the foolish things of the world to confound the wise...and things, which are despised"** (I Cor. 1:26-28).

When the king ordered his men to call on Rahab with reference to the spies, by one act of faith she swallowed her patriotism and lied for the glory of God. She might have been the town heroine; instead she became a heroine of faith. Her faith transcended her patriotism or nationalism. Her faith also proved greater and more honorable than telling the truth— which would have been fatal to the two spies. Based on a legalistic interpretation of the ninth commandment, there are no doubt many who would question Rahab's ethic. Rahab, however, preferred to lose the battle that she might win the war. Had she become the heroine of Jericho, she would never have been heard of again. But she became the heroine of Israel, and her name is held in high esteem to the present day.

Instead of making a deal with the king of Jericho, she pulled off a deal with the two spies. First, she led the king's agents on a wild goose chase. **"Yes, those two men did come here. But they left only a few moments ago. If you hurry you can catch them"** (see Josh. 2:4-5). What in fact had happened was this: She hid the two spies up in the loft. She then pleaded for mercy from the two spies. **"I pray you, swear unto me by the Lord, since I have shewed you kindness, that ye will shew kindness unto my father's house, and give me a true token"** (Josh. 2:12). She even managed to get a deal whereby her parents and brothers and sisters would be spared once the children of Israel made their attack on Jericho (Josh. 2:14). James called this act "justification by works"—his nickname for sanctification, or experimental faith.

The spies agreed and made a historic arrangement with Rahab. These spies came up with an idea that reflected their training at home. They were too young to recall the Passover (and perhaps had not even born then). But they grew up knowing about it and had kept the feast of the Passover every year as long as they could remember. When Rahab had enabled the spies to escape by easing them down from her house on the wall by a scarlet cord, the spies offered this advice reflecting the meaning of the Passover: **"When we come into the land, thou shalt bind this line of scarlet thread in the window which thou didst let us down by: and thou shalt bring thy father, and thy mother, and thy brethren, and all thy father's household, home unto thee...(but) whosoever shall go out of the doors of thy house into the street, his blood shall be upon his head, and we will be guiltless"** (Josh. 2:18-19).

The Scarlet Chord

The scarlet cord, therefore, functioned as the blood had done on the night of the Passover; instead of its being **"when I see the *blood*,"** it was **"when we see the *scarlet cord*, we will pass by you."** The spies returned to the camp of Israel beyond Jordan and reported this story to Joshua. This was received with great joy and as a wonderful confirmation to their faith. **"Truly the Lord hath delivered into our hands all the land; for even all the inhabitants of the country do faint because of us"** (Josh. 2:24).

Not only was this a confirmation of Joshua's faith but also of Rahab's. What a great sense of relief it was to her that she had done the right thing. Not only that; what a wonderful feeling she must have had to know that her shame was transcended by God's grace. For no woman who abuses or cheapens her God-given body can escape that deep, deep feeling of guilt and shame over such carryings on.

Young ladies today will often justify themselves for sleeping with their boyfriends, as will married people make excuse for their secret affairs. They often claim to have no sense of guilt and shame. But this is sheer self-deceit and self-justification. They have much, much shame but refuse to face their truest feelings. Sex outside of marriage, however common in today's society, never builds up the conscience. It is wrong. It is sin. If it is done by a Christian, the result will be God's dealings. If a Christian who experiments with sex outside the marriage bond is not dealt with by God, one must seriously question whether that one is really a Christian after all.

As for Rahab herself, her lifestyle showed she had reached rock bottom. In her lifetime she had gone from virgin to non-virgin; from carnal lust to promiscuity; from promiscuity to prostitution, selling her own body. Rabbinic tradition claimed she was one of the four most beautiful women in the world. But she didn't feel beautiful. She probably had given up all hope of ever feeling pure, good, and useful again. But God has a way of turning things around. God even has a way of making a wrong become right and of turning bad to good. God can turn shame into glory by one stroke of His hand. And He did it with Rahab. She began to feel clean, useful, wanted and respected.

Picture this same Rahab with her mother and father, her brothers and sisters, her nephews and nieces, crowded into that house on the wall (Josh. 2:15). She had secretly persuaded her closest relatives that she was on to something good for a change. She persuaded them. She got them to come along to her house.

In the meantime, Joshua and the children of Israel had crossed over Jordan. The first day they marched around Jericho, blowing their trumpets. Nothing happened. Rahab's family may have begun to get edgy. "What is this? There's no way those people out there can penetrate this walled city." The second day the same crew marched around Jericho, blowing their trumpets. Nothing happened. Rahab's relatives may have grown more tense. But there was one in that house who was holding fast—Rahab. I suspect that the most she did was occasionally walk over to the window to be sure that the scarlet cord was firmly in place. All her eggs were in one basket—that red rope hanging unobtrusively from her window.

Unexpectedly, the children of Israel outside changed their approach. On the seventh day they marched seven times, blowing their trumpets. Suddenly, however, it became deathly quiet. Then it happened. Joshua gave the order: **"SHOUT; FOR THE LORD HATH GIVEN YOU THE CITY."** The people outside shouted. In the twinkling of an eye the walls around the city began to crumble, falling to the ground. The men of war marched in.

Rahab and her family could hear the shrieks and screams of their neighbors, one by one. Would the children of Israel remember? Could the spies have forgotten? Perhaps they had forgotten to give all the details to Joshua? Rahab's entire hope rested on that scarlet cord. The men of war were getting closer as houses all around were being broken into and ransacked. If the spies did indeed forget the arrangement, Rahab's house would surely be the next to be broken into.

But instead of the door being broken down, a firm and majestic knock came at the door. A friendly voice called: "Rahab? Rahab, are you there?" This woman Rahab excitedly answered and opened the door. An armed soldier gestured and kindly ordered, "Step this way, please." With gravest honor and highest dignity, Rahab the harlot, her mother and father, her brothers and sisters, her nephews and nieces, were given a military escort past the fighting and the devastation around them and were brought to permanent safety, never to worry again. **"By faith the harlot Rahab perished not with them that believed not, when she had received the spies with peace."**

Judgment Day had come to Jericho. Judgment Day is coming to London, to Los Angeles, to Tokyo and to every city in the world. There will be shrieks and screams. **"Behold, he cometh with clouds; and every eye shall see him, and they also which pierced him, and all kindreds of the earth shall wail because of him. Even so, Amen" (Rev. 1:7).** When that day comes, there will be one hope: the blood of the same Lord Jesus Christ. Those who have put all their eggs into one basket will not be disappointed. Let the most wicked person who reads these lines—and the most godly—put his trust in what matters. The scarlet cord. That precious blood.

Chapter Twenty-Seven

Gideon and Barak

Hebrews 11:32

And what shall I more say? for the time would fail me to tell of Gideon, and of Barak...

Our writer now wants to wind up his selection of particular personalities of the Old Testament. But he fears that someone might think he is suggesting that only the previously mentioned names are the ones in the Old Testament who had faith. He therefore begins to change the subject by randomly calling out certain people, implying that he could go on and on. Indeed, when he reaches verse 33, he stops mentioning actual names and supplies events, as if to invite *us* to supply the names!

At any rate, our writer wants us to know that there is no end to the list of the incidents that could be mentioned. John felt a similar dilemma: **"There are also many other things which Jesus did, the which, if they should be written every one, I suppose that even the world itself could not contain the books that should be written" (John 21:25).** Mentioning particular names in Hebrews 11:32, our writer expects us to fill in the events. Surely by now, he seems to think, we ought to know him well enough to figure out what he has in mind when he mentions Gideon, Barak and others.

Our own method in these closing chapters will be to combine two names at a time until we are forced to go from individual persons to the universal principles that the events of verses 34-40 uphold. Pairing two men in this and the next two chapters is not entirely arbitrary, for a helpful pattern develops that makes such a pairing quite useful. Gideon and Barak were weak men. Samson and Jephthah were strong men. David and Samuel were great men.

Our writer moves from the Book of Joshua to the Book of Judges. When Moses died, God raised up his successor Joshua. For reasons we cannot understand, the Lord raised up no successor to Joshua. It is a curious thing, not infrequently seen in history, that God provides no successor equal to a man He clearly had raised up. Melanchthon wasn't the man Luther was, but he gave Lutheranism its complexion. Beza wasn't the man Calvin was, but he gave Calvinism its complexion. Whitefield had no successor. Spurgeon had no successor.

Two possible explanations can be given for why God would allow this curious non-phenomenon: (1) that men left without strong leadership will see what they are in themselves, and (2) that they will appreciate strong leadership when they have it. What is sadder than a generation without leadership? Only this: a generation full of small men who scramble for leadership for which they are not prepared (either at a natural or spiritual level). Perhaps our generation is like that of the Judges: We are experiencing a dearth of greatness upon the horizon when every man does **"that which is right in his own eyes"** (Judges 17:6).

For three hundred years following Joshua, God provided no truly *great* leader but only what are called **"judges."** The judges were apparently raised up to arbitrate in the affairs of men (e.g., civil or domestic quarrels) and to provide military leadership against impending enemies. Only a handful of these judges have much stature in Old Testament history.

During this period of time the twelve tribes of Israel, now dwelling in Canaan, were independent tribes under a confederacy. They had failed to utterly wipe out all the Canaanites, and this failure turned out to be the reason for their endless troubles. The Canaanites proved to be their constant enemies. At the root of the Israelites' malady was this: They forgot God. They began to make themselves at home in Canaan without remembering who gave them their land. They began to live as though nature was all there was. They ceased to be offended by strange gods in the land and were themselves soon given to idolatry.

Why Barak Made Faith's Hall of Fame

Our curiosity compels us at once to ask, "Why is Barak included in this list of heroes of the faith?" The story of Barak is really about Deborah. Yet it is Barak who gets his name mentioned in our "faith" chapter. Why? The answer is one of no small encouragement to us, who by nature are anything but strong people.

We must begin with Deborah. She was one of the judges that God raised up in Israel. That God should raise up a woman to a position of power tells us a lot about the men of the day. It was a time when Israel was in a deplorable state of affairs. God was grieved. But people finally began to cry to Him for help (Judges 4:3). Why? Because the Lord had given them over to a fierce, cruel neighbor, to Jabin, the king of Canaan. The captain of the Canaanite army was a man named Sisera. Sisera had 900 chariots of iron—a formidable type of weaponry and means of transportation. He had been a source of oppression for twenty years—a long time to have bad neighbors.

Deborah had been given a message from the Lord regarding Sisera: **"I will deliver him into thine hand" (Judges 4:7).** She summoned Barak to take ten thousand men to Mount Tabor for the purpose of defeating Sisera in war. Barak, however, was not so anxious to become a military hero—or martyr. His reply to Deborah was this: **"If thou wilt *go with me*, then I will go: but if thou wilt not go with me, then I will not go" (Judges 4:8).**

Deborah went along with this condition, but gave this warning to Barak: **"I will surely go with thee: notwithstanding the journey that thou takest shall not be for thine honor; for the Lord shall sell Sisera into the hand of a woman" (Judges 4:9).** In other words, Barak will go down in history as having had to share his moment of glory with a woman! It is to Deborah's great credit that she was sensitive to masculine pride. This **"mother in Israel,"** as she came to be known (Judges 5:7), was not a feminist; she was a godly woman.

Barak seems to have grasped all the implications. But he was determined not to go without Deborah at his side. **"And Deborah arose, and went with Barak to Kedesh" (Judges 4:9).** With Deborah at his side Barak achieved a marvelous victory. The result: **"All the host of Sisera fell upon the edge of the sword; and there was not a man left" (Judges 4:16).** It was a very happy ending indeed. Judges 5 records the Song of Deborah and Barak, ending with these words: **"The land had rest forty years" (v. 31).**

Why is Barak's faith mentioned? There are two reasons. First, God does not ask us to impute to ourselves more faith than is there. Paul admonishes each of us **"not to think of himself more highly than he ought to think; but to think soberly, according as God hath dealt to every man the measure of faith" (Rom. 12:3).** God doesn't ask us to elevate ourselves to the level of our incompetence (the Peter Principle), nor does He ask us to tempt Him by acting as if we had a gift or an ability which we haven't got.

It takes great faith to have a realistic appraisal of yourself. There are many miserable Christians who could be rid of their misery if they began to **"think soberly"** about themselves. Barak simply knew he couldn't do what Deborah asked him to do without her at his side. It takes grace to admit to such dependence. It takes grace to say, "I don't have this (or that) gift. I'm sorry. I can't do it." That is faith. For it is living within the **"measure"** of one's faith. Too many of us are like the reckless child who said, "Look, Mom, no hands; look, Mom, no teeth!"—but who still refuses to admit to any limitations or miscalculations.

However, the second and chief reason Barak's faith was mentioned is this: He never wanted personal glory in the first place. Deborah's warning did not threaten him. It played right into his godly desire to see a victory for Israel over Sisera. That is what Barak wanted—nothing more. Personal glory was never in his mind. This made him a hero after all. A hero of faith.

A Weak Man who Believed God

Though Gideon is much better known than Barak, by nature he was certainly no stronger than Barak. Gideon, too, was a weak man. His secret was not the way he felt about himself, but what God saw in him.

The situation was this: After the forty years of rest that came as a result of Barak's and Deborah's victory, a people called the Midianites had developed the rather nasty habit of annually destroying Israel's crops at about the very time they were ripe. This they did for seven years. **"And Israel was greatly impoverished because of the Midianites; and the children of Israel cried unto the Lord" (Judges 6:6).**

Gideon was found threshing wheat by the winepress and hiding it from the Midianites. An angel in disguise appeared to him (another reminder of Hebrews 13:2) with the surprising message that God had raised him up to defeat the Midianites. Gideon's response, after initially quarreling with the angel over Israel's plight, was to complain. He referred to the lack of class in his family background and to the fact that he himself was the weakest of his family. (Our writer would be impressed with this.)

Although the Lord promised to be with him, this promise wasn't quite enough for Gideon. He made this request: **"If now I have found grace in thy sight, then shew me a sign that thou talkest with me" (Judges 6:17).** This wasn't such an unreasonable request; Gideon simply wanted to know that it was truly God who was speaking to him. Gideon got his sign; after making meat and unleavened cakes for the angel, **"there rose up fire out of the rock and consumed the flesh and the unleavened cakes."** Gideon said, **"Alas, 0 Lord God! for I have seen an angel of the Lord face to face" (Judges 6:21-22).**

Gideon is to be excused for having wanted to be sure it was really God who promised to use him. Indeed, God understood and gave Gideon an undeniable, external confirmation of his faith—enough, surely, to confirm his faith in God forever. One would think that this man Gideon would never doubt God again, but he did. Gideon ought never to have questioned God's favor again, but he did. He ought never to have needed more assurance that he was raised up by the Lord, but he did. He ought never again to have gone back to God and asked for yet another indication that he was God's man for the hour. But he did. What followed was Gideon's famous fleece. **"Gideon said unto God, If thou wilt save Israel by mine hand, as thou hast said, Behold, I will put a fleece of wool in the floor; and if the dew be on the fleece only, and it be dry upon all the earth** beside, *then shall I* **know that thou wilt save Israel by mine hand"** **(Judges 6:36-37).** God accommodated Gideon's request. The next day he got a bowl full of water out of the fleece. Surely that unusual occurrence would remove all doubt, but it didn't. Gideon was sure it would—**"then shall I know."** But he didn't **"know"** as he thought he would. Gideon was beginning to get self-conscious before the Lord. **"Let not thine anger be hot against me, and I will speak but this once: let me prove, I pray thee, but this once with the fleece; let it now be—dry only upon the fleece, and upon all the ground let there be dew" (Judges 6:40).** The next day the fleece was dry, and there was dew all over the ground.

What amazes me is that God accommodated Gideon with the very sign he wanted. First one way, then in reverse—just as he asked. God might easily have dropped this weak, doubting man by refusing to put up with any more of this nonsense and by looking elsewhere for a man—a man who would believe God the first time. But God stayed with Gideon. God saw in Gideon a diamond in the rough and called him a **"mighty man of valor" (Judges 6:12)** before he even had a chance to live up to such imputed strength! Gideon eventually achieved one of the most memorable victories over Israel's enemies to be found in all Holy Writ. It is that victory which our writer may actually have had in mind.

In any case, Gideon and Barak are examples of weak men that God graciously and mightily used. If God can use Gideon and Barak, He can use anybody. I cannot think of a more encouraging thought than that.

Chapter Twenty-Eight

Samson and Jephtath?

Hebrews 11:32

And what shall I more say? for the time would fail me to tell of...Samson, and of Jephthae...

Our two men in this chapter were strong men; one had brains (Jephthah), the other had brawn (Samson). Jephthah was a rugged outcast of Israel whose intellectual leadership was suddenly needed; Samson was a powerful specimen of humanity who pulled up by the roots everything that annoyed him or got in his way. There is yet another thing that these two had in common: an ugly blemish on their lives that is better remembered than their faith.

If the writer of the Epistle to the Hebrews had not mentioned them, who among us would have thought to do so? Most of us think of the blemishes of Samson and Jephthah, and consequently do not see their faith. Our writer was not a legalist; he could see past their blemishes.

Yet it is a fact of life that people tend to remember the bad rather than the good. Neville Chamberlain is still remembered for one thing primarily: his failure to recognize Hitler for what he was. Richard Nixon will be remembered primarily for Watergate. But our writer wants us to look at Samson and Jephthah, not for their mistakes, but for their example as men of faith. It is again our job to fill in the blanks and surmise what the writer might have said about these two men.

A Hero who Shunned the Mainstream

One of the more interesting things that emerge from the account of Jephthah is the question of the "mainstream." What is the mainstream? All of us—whatever our Christian tradition or background—tend to think that *we* are in the mainstream of Christianity. A mainstream is defined as "a river with tributaries"; figuratively, it is the "chief direction or trend." Who then is the mainstream of Christianity? The Roman Catholics think they are. Members of the Church of England think they are. Those following the Reformed tradition think they are, via Calvin and Augustine. The Mennonites and certain Baptists think they are, via the Anabaptists and Donatists.

I know a man who is *sure* that he is in the mainstream. He has forecast that if revival ever comes, it will come first to America. By America, he means the state of Kentucky. By Kentucky, he means Ashland, Kentucky. By Ashland, Kentucky, he means a certain street and certain address in Ashland. Though we may scoff at this man's rather self-centered prediction, *all of us* feel—or want to feel—that we are the true heirs of the Apostles, whatever tradition we may lay claim to.

One thing is certain about Jephthah, though: He was clearly not in the mainstream. But that is what our writer would like about him. Our writer delights in focusing on the torch of God's glory being passed to the unexpected. Jephthah was the son of a prostitute and consequently, he was disinherited (see Judges 11:2). Worst of all, Jephthah attracted the scum of the earth.

While Jephthah was obviously a born leader, he attracted only those nobody else wanted. This made him immensely unattractive to the "mainstream" of ancient Israel. Nobody that "mattered" took any notice of Jephthah and his band. Jephthah and his followers were avoided like the plague. One might also add that Jephthah himself probably grew up with a chip on his shoulder. After all, he had a bad start in life and grew up feeling rejected.

But I wish to give a slightly different definition of "mainstream." It is that to which God turns and through whom He is pleased to manifest Himself. It tends, by the way, to be **"outside the camp."** Our Lord Jesus Christ was not exactly in the mainstream of His day. He suffered **"without the gate"** that He might sanctify His people with His own blood. **"Let us go forth therefore unto Him without the camp, bearing His reproach" (Heb. 13:12-13).** When God turns to a particular body of men, it often takes everybody else by surprise. God has a way of making the unlikely and the unexpected the center of His most recent activity.

Everybody knew about Jephthah but nobody that "mattered" called on him—for anything. Until one day. When the children of Israel were absolutely desperate, they turned to the scum of the earth for help. This they did when the children of Ammon made war against Israel (Judges 11:4-5). They even made Jephthah their captain; he was in a strategic bargaining position and had the whole of Israel on their knees begging to him. Jephthah's first task would be to forgive the world and get that chip off his shoulder. At any rate the mainstream was now Jephthah's leadership and command. The torch was passed to him. Suddenly he was the wave of the future.

But what was Jephthah's faith? It was a brilliant understanding of God's purpose in history. Jephthah may have been an outcast in Israel, but he knew his history. He had done his homework. Never underestimate this—that God uses knowledge. We are told that Stephen spoke with such authority that **"they were not able to resist the wisdom and the spirit by which he spake" (Acts 6:10). "Sanctify the Lord God in your hearts: and be ready always to give an answer to every man that asketh you a reason of the hope that is in you with meekness and fear" (I Pet. 3:15).**

Jephthah put his enemies to shame by his knowledge of God's purpose in history. What happened was this: The king of Ammon picked a quarrel with Israel concerning an event which had taken place three hundred years before; he accused Israel of stealing their land. Did the king of Ammon have a point? Not at all, argued Jephthah. Point by point, Jephthah traced every step of the children of Israel from the time they left Egypt. When Israel was attacked, God gave them power to defend themselves. Furthermore, it was the *Lord God* who dispossessed the Amorites; who would want to fight against such a God?

Jephthah also argued that since Israel had already been in the land for three hundred years, why should the king of Ammon suddenly be getting anxious about a matter that his predecessors took no notice of? Jephthah concluded that God should be the One to judge the whole matter (see Judges 11:1-27).

That was Jephthah's faith; he was mastered by the truth.

I wish I could end the story of Jephthah there. But I cannot. I refer to that awful blemish in Jephthah—what everyone remembers and undoubtedly one of the strangest and most foolish acts of pre-Watergate history. Jephthah was a strong man and a great thinker. A man's genius is usually his downfall. Every man has his blind spot. Said Calvin: "In every saint there is always to be found something reprehensible." Jephthah made a vow—a foolish, needless vow: If God would truly defeat the enemy, he would give Him a human sacrifice. Who would it be? The first person he met at his house (Judges 11:30-31).

God gave Jephthah the victory. But not because of the vow. The victory was already assured by Jephthah's own brilliant argument. But Jephthah began to doubt his own word. He felt this need to make a vow. A vow is nature's way of robbing God of His glory. Vows do the very opposite of what people think they do. A vow is concocted not because of the Spirit's directive, but because it makes us feel better. We then take the fact that we feel better as the Spirit's witness that we are on the right track. We project that good feeling upon the backdrop of God's heart and claim it as His will, when it is almost always nothing but our own unbelief dressed in self-righteous apparel.

The clearest hint for all ages regarding vows and God's will is to be seen in Jephthah's case. First, when it came into his mind to make a vow, God rebuked his unbelief by letting him make a foolish vow. Second, the seal of God's disapproval was in letting Jephthah's own daughter be the first to walk through those doors of his own house. Jephthah's greatest folly yet is in thinking he had to keep this silly vow.

One may argue that the Law says one must keep any vow one makes (see Deut. 23:21). I answer: The Law is not of faith (Gal. 3:12). Jephthah showed himself a man of faith when he disputed with the king; he showed himself a foolish legalist when it came to trusting the very God he had exalted. Legalistic thinking can lead people to do crazy things. It is amazing how one can be brilliant in one area of Christian living and utterly blind in another!

I offer this advice regarding vows (other than the marriage vow and the vow to be a Christian): Don't make them. And if you have already made them, forget them. As to God's revealed direction, don't make vows—simply keep His word. You are bound to His Word before you make a vow. When you vow to do what the Bible has already commanded, you become your own kind of mediator. And if you vow to do something *not* clearly revealed in the Bible, you are self-righteously upstaging God's righteousness (this is why vows often lead to the grossest bondage).

A HERO whOSE DEATH WAS his FINEST HOUR

Unlike Jephthah, Samson not only had a respectable birth but was the product of godly parents. Our writer would not want us to think that the torch of God's glory is passed only to the unpredictable. The Lord said to Samson's mother: **"Thou shalt conceive, and bear a son; and no razor shall come on his head: for the child shall be a Nazarite unto God from the womb: and he shall begin to deliver Israel out of the hand of the Philistines" (Judges 13:5).**

This was not a vow which Samson's mother made; it was a direct command of God to her. It is not for us to decide why God did this. We only know that He did. It was a test of Samson's parents' faith that they honored God's word to them, but it was also a test of Samson's own faith.

Samson's never having a haircut was simply the tangible secret of his strength. His faith was drawing from the strength of his secret. This strength was not intellectual like Jephthah's; it was entirely physical. On one occasion a young lion attacked Samson. **"And the Spirit of the Lord came mightily upon him, and he rent him as he would have rent a kid, and he had nothing in his hand" (Judges 14:5-6).**

Seeking vengeance on another occasion, **"Samson went and caught three hundred foxes, and took firebrands, and turned tail to tail, and put a firebrand in the midst between two tails. And when he had set the brands on fire, he let them go into the standing corn of the Philistines, and burnt up both the shocks, and also the standing corn, with the vineyards and olives"** (Judges 15:4-5).

This event "made" Samson in the eyes of Israel. He permitted himself to be bound by his own people and delivered to the Philistines. **"The Spirit of the Lord came mightily upon him, and the cords that were upon his arms became as flax that was burnt with fire, and his bands loosed from off his hands. And he found a new jawbone of an ass and put forth his hand, and took it, and slew a thousand men therewith"** (Judges 15:14-15). Samson was then made one of the judges of Israel, which he judged for twenty years.

We might wish we could end the story there, but we cannot. We have noted that man's genius is usually his downfall. Jephthah was brilliant— and so foolish. Samson was a man's man—virile, masculine and handsome. But he had a terrible weakness: women. It will be recalled that Barak had a different kind of weakness. Neither Samson nor Barak had a truly healthy attitude towards women. Barak had a mother-fixation (or something like that) for Deborah; Samson treated women as things.

Yet, the examples of Barak and Samson also show that God can use all kinds of men. The degree of a man's sexuality, insofar as his usefulness is concerned, is largely irrelevant. But one with a high degree of sexuality is much more vulnerable and is in a potentially dangerous state. The tendency of the latter also is sometimes to treat the opposite sex as things, or objects.

Samson treated Delilah as an object. Had he loved her in a healthy way, he would have married her. Secondly, he would have won her respect and confidence. But Samson neither married Delilah nor won her respect. So she felt that she owed him nothing, and she made herself available to the highest bidder. The highest bid: 1,100 pieces of silver. The deal: to find the secret of Samson's strength.

It is to the credit of this judge in Israel that he succeeded in rejecting Delilah's pressure as long as he did. He lied to her three times when she tried to find out the secret of his great strength. He ought to have rejected her the first time she started prying into his secret. But his weakness for Delilah overruled his judgment. Delilah had two weapons: her body and her nagging; she used both to the fullest extent. **"She pressed him daily with her words, and urged him, so that his soul was vexed unto death"** (Judges 16:16).

What followed can be put in six of the saddest words of Scripture: **"He told her all his heart"** (Judges 16:17). Picture now this sad scene. Rugged Samson, at the height of his career but now a fallen leader in Israel, lying pitifully on the lap of Delilah—fast asleep. The moment she had been waiting for had arrived. The shears were at her fingertips, and she began cutting away.

When Samson woke up, he felt no different. He realized what she had done, but he felt fine. **"I will go out as at other times before, and shake myself"** (Judges 16:20). It is the way any backslider feels at first—no different. Many backsliders at first refuse to acknowledge their sin on the basis that they don't feel a thing. The backslider is always filled with his own ways (Prov. 14:14). Samson didn't feel a thing. **"He wist not that the Lord was departed from him"** (Judges 16:20).

But he found out soon enough. **"Be sure your sin will find you out"** (Num. 32:23). The Philistines captured him. Samson was as weak as a kitten. He couldn't do what he had always done before. The Philistines ruthlessly put out his two eyes, bound him with fetters of brass, and put him in prison. Once mightily used, now useless, blind Samson was locked up helplessly in prison. He was left there with nothing to do but think. Thinking over one's folly can be the most torturous kind of punishment. He must have asked himself a thousand times: "How could a man like me get into a mess like this?" The shame of it all: He was a disappointment to his parents, his friends, his countrymen—and to the God who had called him.

"Oh, for one more chance!" I suspect this lamentable piece of flesh now cried from within. How could this pitiful man ever be used again?

With God nothing shall be impossible. Samson's hair began to grow. One day three thousand Philistines decided to throw a party. They were eating and drinking. Then, running out of things to do, they decided to send for Samson, that they might laugh at him. They happened to set him between two giant pillars. Samson whispered a request to a lad nearby, **"Suffer me that I may feel the pillars...that I may lean upon them"** **(Judges 16:26).**

While three thousand were laughing, Samson was praying for one more chance. He took hold of the two middle pillars. He felt a surging within—a familiar strength he had once known but which he feared he would never feel again. The foundations began to quake. **"LET ME DIE WITH THE PHILISTINES,"** he cried. The columns were dislodged; huge stones began to fall. Samson was crushed to death and three thousand Philistines with him.

Samson's death was his finest hour. **"So the dead which he slew at his death were more than they which he slew in his life" (Judges 16:30).** In one moment he was simultaneously restored and used. "All's well that ends well," the saying goes. Samson, whose glory had turned to shame, was given grace by the most high God to leave this world in a burst of reclaimed glory.

Chapter Twenty-Nine

David and Samuel

Hebrews 11:32

And what shall I more say? for the time would fail me to tell of...David also, and Samuel...

We have had occasion more than once in our study of the stalwarts of Hebrews 11 to mention the matter of greatness, or rather the dearth of greatness, in the world today. Few there are whose manner of life and quality of mind give the impression of greatness. I fear this is true, whether in the realm of politics or religion. It is our privilege in this study to examine greatness at close range. I hope that one contribution from the present chapter will be that of giving the reader some idea what greatness is. We continue with Hebrews 11:32 in which our writer has begun to wind up his "faith" chapter. Gideon and Barak were weak men. Samson and Jephthah were strong men. David and Samuel were great men.

We may ask: What is a small man? We need not look very far to find one. He has a distorted sense of ambition, thinking entirely of himself, his own career, and especially his name. He is not ambitious for principle (unless it coincides with what will advance him personally) but for position—a position of power and prestige. Such a man seldom has much objectivity about himself. If he is forced to see himself as he truly is, he shrugs his shoulders and says, "But who isn't like this?" He tends to impute to himself more ability than is there and almost always personifies the "Peter Principle"—promoting himself to the level of his incompetence. He has convinced himself that true greatness does not exist. This is his justification for his unrestrained greed.

There isn't one small man in Hebrews 11. Faith does not breed smallness. Faith engenders realistic thinking about oneself. Faith brings a person to accept himself as he is and then not to impute to himself one whit more than God has been pleased to give him. **"I had rather be a doorkeeper in the house of my God, than to dwell in the tents of wickedness" (Psa. 84:10).**

True greatness is to be found when three ingredients coincide—genius, integrity, crisis. The omission of any of these probably removes the possibility of greatness. For example, genius and integrity may be present in one person, but if a crisis does not emerge to bring out the greatness, it is never discovered. It may be argued that such a person is truly great nonetheless. I answer: Unless there is a crisis to prove it, the matter of genius and integrity is mostly conjecture. Must the element of genius be present? By greatness I do not merely mean magnanimity; I refer also to a quality of mind that God has given to one.

Samuel and David were strategic figures in Israel's transition period from the era of the judges to the kings. Samuel was the greatest figure since Moses. He marks the end of one era and the beginning of another. He was the last of the judges; the first of a new breed of prophets. David was Israel's greatest king and pre-figured Messiah more than any other. These two men had greatness in common because each was motivated by a detachment from earthly vindication and glory, and that was their faith.

Samuel's Greatness

Samuel refused to fall prey to Israel's bandwagon syndrome. The people said, **"We want a king over us" (I Sam. 8:19).** They wanted a king so that they could be like other nations. But this request for a king flew in the face of God's own design for Israel **"to be a special people unto Himself, above all people that are upon the face of the earth" (Deut. 7:6).** The desire for a king, then, showed how much the children of Israel had degenerated spiritually. There is no clearer sign of backsliding than the desire to be like the world. For those who have become like the world have lost their Christian identity.

Samuel was unimpressed by this popular trend and warned against it. Apart from vast spiritual implications, Samuel showed them that, even pragmatically speaking, their having a king was a bad move. For there would be economic disadvantages and new sets of problems that would work against the happiness of the life they already had. He therefore gave this prophecy: **"Ye shall cry out in that day because of your king which ye shall have chosen you; and the Lord will not hear you in that day" (I Sam. 8:18).** But the people were adamant. **"Nay; but we will have a king over us" (I Sam. 8:19).** Samuel's first great crisis had arrived.

Samuel did not take it personally when his leadership was rejected. This is one of the tests of greatness. Small men always take rejection personally. Knowing that he had followed the Lord's will, Samuel could safely conclude that what the people did was due to their own disobedience to God. Had he taken the rejection of his counsel personally, he would have said, "You folks just don't appreciate me. I resign."

Samuel could see that they needed him more than ever, even if *they* did not see this. Samuel also knew that *God* needed him to be where he was at the time. It would have been very easy for him to say, "I'm no use to these stiff-necked people. Let them get what's coming to them." Many able men miss greatness only because they cannot handle rejection. Samuel's greatest trial and triumph at this pivotal moment in Israel's history was to act responsibly before God and men when his advice went unheeded.

What did Samuel do next? He actually went to great pains to find Israel a king. Samuel was the first kingmaker. Why did Samuel help them to do what he had told them they ought not to do? Because God had told him to. That was enough. This was Samuel's integrity—pleasing God. A small man could never have done what Samuel did. One symptom of smallness is inflexibility. Samuel, however, wasn't doing it for them; it was for God. Neither did he say to them, "I'm not doing this for you but for God." He was too big to act like that. He began looking for a king as though the idea was his own. After all, it was now God's own will. **"The**

**Lord said to Samuel, Hearken unto their voice, and make them a king"
(I Sam. 8:22).**

Samuel's greatness is traceable to the fact that he never forgot the
manner of his own calling. It all began when he said to God, **"Speak,
Lord; for thy servant heareth" (I Sam. 3:9).** Samuel was true to the voice
of God from then on. He lived by that voice. He never outgrew the need of
that voice. Many good and potentially great men go astray because, at
some point along the way, they abandon the simplicity of following the
voice of God that began their career. Samuel never did that.

Samuel's discovery of Saul was the consequence of the former's most
meticulous search for the best man available at the time. But Saul went
wrong. **"I gave thee a king in mine anger, and took him away in my
wrath" (Hosea 13:11).** A rather conspicuous omission in Hebrews 11:32 is
Saul. Our writer went from Samuel to David.

It is difficult to know precisely what our writer might have specifically
said about Samuel. It could well have been the way in which Samuel found
David. God said to Samuel that He wanted **"a man after His own heart" (I
Sam. 13:14).** When Samuel came to Jesse to find a successor to Saul, the
Lord said: **"Look not on his countenance, or on the height of his stature;
because I have refused him: for the Lord seeth not as man seeth; for
man looketh on the outward appearance, but the Lord looketh on the
heart" (I Sam. 16:7).**

To everyone's surprise Samuel chose David. **"And the Lord said,
Arise, anoint him: for this is he" (I Sam. 16:12).** Samuel's greatness was
in his refusal to be vindicated by contemporary opinion. Faith seeks its vindication from God only.

Though it may have been hard for Samuel to go along with Israel's
request for a king, he did so because *God told him to.* It may have been hard
for Samuel to reject the sons of Jesse who outwardly seemed more quali-
fied; but he chose David because *God told him to.* That was the pattern of
Samuel's life. It was the source of his greatness.

WHEN A HERO SINS

The life of David was so vast that one might come up with thirty or forty events in his career that could be explained only in terms of faith. Which of these would our writer have selected?

If we were surprised that Samson was listed as a man of faith, we might be equally surprised that David is mentioned when we think of the tragic sins he committed. Yet this is the sort of thing our writer could have had in mind, for he delights in showing the triumph of faith over human frailty. David was a truly great man, but he experienced a fall so tragic that no human calculation would have predicted his usefulness to God again. But the fact that Bathsheba's child was put in the Messianic line proves God's grace.

We have had occasion already to refer to Matthew's genealogy (the mention of Rahab in Matthew 1:5). The subject of the continuity of Abraham's seed has had considerable prominence in the "faith" chapter, and the subject of genealogy is therefore most relevant. As for Matthew's genealogy, it normally does not offer any details other than to show the direct continuity of Messiah's seed itself. But in Matthew 1:6 we read: **"And Jesse begat David the king; and David the king begat Solomon** *of her that had been the wife of Urias.*" Why did Matthew bother to throw in that last part? I think it represents the same sort of thinking that our writer has evidenced in Hebrews 11.

The first big question is, how could a man after God's own heart sink so low? David, having come to the prime of life and the pinnacle of his career, fell into temptation and then sin. The situation was this: While Joab's army was in the heat of battle, David stayed behind in Jerusalem. After an afternoon nap, David walked outside on his roof. Not far away, David noticed a beautiful woman, washing herself. Rather than resist the urge, David had his men find out more about her. The information came back. Her name: Bathsheba. Father: Eliam. Husband: Uriah, a soldier in battle.

That last bit of information should certainly have stopped David. But it didn't. He sent for her, and she came. He lay with her. Whether this would have been a one-time encounter or a continued affair, we don't know. But we do know that a problem developed. Bathsheba had conceived, and a baby was on the way.

David had what he thought was an ingenious solution. He sent for Uriah and gave him a weekend to spend time with his wife. Bathsheba's pregnancy was in such an early stage that Uriah would never have questioned whether it was his baby. But things didn't go as planned. David could not have known that Uriah would develop a guilt complex; Uriah couldn't bring himself to enjoy his wife while his fellow-soldiers were in battle.

When David got word of this, he knew that he was in deep trouble. Things went from bad to worse. David now made a most cowardly and unthinkable decision: He put Uriah in the front line of the next battle, where Uriah would most likely be killed. He was. It gave David temporary relief—until a man by the name of Nathan brought home David's sin (II Sam. 12:1-13). David's reaction was self-righteous at first, but when his own sin was clearly exposed, he was laid low.

If anyone wants to know how a man after God's own heart reacts after his sin has been brought home, he should read Psalm 51. The key verse is this: **"Against Thee, Thee only, have I sinned, and done this evil in Thy sight: that Thou mightest be justified when Thou speakest, and be clear when Thou judgest" (Psa. 51:4).** This psalm is an affirmation of God's justice, God's righteousness, God's vindication. David continued: **"Cast me not away from Thy presence; and take not Thy Holy Spirit from me" (v. 11).** He did not say, "Don't take my kingdom from me." At the bottom of David's sorrow was the knowledge he had failed God. David's sin revealed where his heart really was. He did not justify himself and accuse God; he accused himself and justified God.

The secret of David's greatness, then, was a direct relationship between his own heart and God's. David sinned again when he numbered the people. He was offered the choice of three punishments. He had one response: **"I am in a great strait: let us fall now into the hand of the Lord; for his mercies are great: and let me not fall into the hand of man" (II Sam. 24:14).** He was governed by his relationship with God. What motivated David was not his own kingdom and glory but rather the fact of Messiah's kingdom. He looked forward to Messiah's kingdom.

David wanted to build the Temple. When he was told that he could not do it, it was all right with him. He never saw his own kingdom as final; he looked beyond. Like Samuel he was detached from a need of earthly vindication. He delighted in God's heavenly glory. David was Israel's greatest king because he, more than any other, delighted in God's ways and God's glory. The more men set their sights on God's glory, the more useful they are to men on earth. What a contrast today when one looks at leaders in the world.

As Samuel's greatness is traceable to his calling, so David's greatness is to be seen long before he became king of Israel. At a time when the whole of Israel was terrified, David, who had been secretly anointed king, became the unexpected hero. Israel was in terror because of the giant Goliath who stood nine feet and six inches tall. Goliath had been shouting constantly across the meadow to the Israelites, blaspheming Israel's God. He challenged them to send one of their own men to face him, but of course none would do this.

When David heard of this, he was appalled that there was such an utter lack of faith among the soldiers. David simply saw Goliath as an uncircumcised Philistine. When nobody would accept Goliath's challenge, David did. He might have thought, "I must not make myself too vulnerable. After all, I'm the future king of Israel. If Goliath should injure or kill me, there go my chances of being king." Thinking like that never entered David's mind. He shouted to Goliath, **"Thou comest to me with a sword, and with a spear, and with a shield: but I come to thee in the name of the Lord of hosts, the God of the armies of Israel, whom thou hast defied" (I Sam. 17:45).** With one smooth stone David knocked Goliath unconscious, then took Goliath's own sword and cut off his head. David was neither afraid of Goliath nor did he feel a need to protect himself.

It was that spirit in David that carried him not only to the throne, but to the greatness for which he is known. True greatness consists in not loving one's own life. David was detached from a need to vindicate himself. That was the secret of his greatness and that was his faith. He was so certain of the power and will of God that he lost sight of himself.

Greatness will continue to elude the latter part of the twentieth century as long as men are full of themselves. Faith is a self-emptying grace. Samuel had it—David had it. Do we have it?

Chapter Thirty

The Prophets and "Others"

Hebrews 11:32-38

And what shall I more say? for the time would fail me to tell of...the prophets...and others...

The writer of Hebrews makes a passing reference to **"the prophets"** in Hebrews 11:32, but doesn't give us much of a clue as to which prophets he has in mind. Does he mean men like Jeremiah and Isaiah? Is he speaking of all those who have a book in their name in the Old Testament canon? Does Hebrews 11:33-38 refer only to what these **"prophets"** did?

Who are the prophets our writer is referring to? A plausible case might be made that Elijah and Elisha are who he is referring to. For as Barak, Gideon, Samson, and Jephthah are described in the Book of Judges, Samuel in I Samuel, and David in I and II Samuel, perhaps our writer was moving right along in the canon and came to Elijah in I Kings and Elisha in II Kings. The reference in Hebrews 11:35 to women who **"received their dead raised to life" (v. 35)** clearly relates to Elijah and Elisha (see I Kings 17:22 and II Kings 4:35).

Quenching **"the violence of fire,"** mentioned in Hebrews 11:34, would appear to describe Shadrach, Meshach and Abednego, who were found walking alive in the fiery furnace (see Daniel 3:25), though they are not normally regarded as prophets. Daniel, who **"stopped the mouths of lions"** **(v. 33)**, certainly was a prophet. The mention of being **"sawn asunder"** **(v. 37)** may refer to an event in the Maccabean period.

Who then is a prophet? Samuel is often regarded as the first prophet of his kind. However, Moses and Enoch had certainly been prophets before him. Even Abel was a prophet (Luke 11:50-51). The Apostle John said that **"the testimony of Jesus is the spirit of prophecy"** **(Revelation 19:10)**. According to Joel both **"sons and daughters shall prophesy"** **(Joel 2:28)**.

If our writer is speaking of prophets in a very narrow sense, he presumably means men like Elijah and Elisha and most certainly those whose books are included in the Old Testament canon. If a broader meaning can be placed on what he means by **"the prophets,"** it would include *all Christians*—everyone who has a vital relationship with God. Our writer was wanting to encourage all who read his epistle, not just the "clergy." The priests of the Old Testament were the "clergy" of their day. Prophets, on the other hand, usually lacked proper ministerial credentials.

However, we do not need to worry if the meaning our writer intends by his reference to prophets is not resolved. Much less should any of us feel that we are excluded from the possibilities of faith described in Hebrews 11. For the writer of Hebrews ultimately comes up with a word that includes all of us: **"others."** These unnamed "other" heroes are mentioned in verses 35 and 36. Thank God for this reference to *others*! This is where you and I surely come in.

If I thought that the possibilities of faith outlined in Hebrews 11 were limited to a certain generation or to only those illustrious people mentioned, it would be somewhat demoralizing rather than encouraging to read this great faith chapter. What inspires me to read it again and again is the very possibility that I can do what they did. How? Because I serve the same God. **"Jesus Christ the same yesterday, and today, and for ever"** **(Hebrews 13:8)**. At any rate, we need not figure out precisely who our writer was referring to in Hebrews 11:33-38 in order to glean principles which may be applied to our lives today.

The Unique Possibilities of Faith

There are three lessons to be found in Hebrews 11:33-35:

1. *True faith is always original.* This is partly what I mean by the "unique" possibilities of faith. True faith is never an imitation. The same God who loves each person as though there were no one else to love also challenges each person as if there were no one else who could succeed. True faith challenges us to be unique and to set our own pace.

The Bible was not given to the church to set limits on what the church can do—much less to limit "the extraordinary" to biblical times. Though the Bible is meant to correct us in case we err doctrinally, the faith it inspires is designed to release us to do in our generation what the people of the Bible (and the heroes of church history) did in theirs. The challenge to uniqueness emancipates us from being intimidated by yesterday's successes or failures. The freedom for uniqueness allows us to be ourselves and not have to imitate other people or be conformed to what they try to make us.

What emerges as a common thread in the events described in Hebrews 11:33-35 is that they were *unprecedented.* When Daniel was thrown into the lions' den, there was no precedent for his coming out alive. Yet his faith **"stopped the mouths of lions."** It might be added that this is something that seems not to have happened since! Likewise, when Shadrach, Meshach and Abednego were bound and cast into the fiery furnace, there was no precedent that they would be seen walking loose with the Fourth Man. But their faith **"quenched the violence of fire."**

When Hezekiah was told to set his house in order because his death was imminent, he had every reason to believe it. But he refused to believe it; he **"obtained a promise,"** and fifteen years were added to his life. **"Out of weakness he was made strong."**

Faith, then, is original. It sets its own pace and loves to treat existing molds with contempt. It mocks precedents and transcends our own projections. Moreover, the originality of faith is often preserved; that is, God seems to actually keep others from doing the same thing.

The originality of faith is preserved if only to prohibit us from basing our personal expectations on a precedent. Like Joshua's extraordinary day, **"There was no day like that before it or after it" (Joshua 10:14)**.

2. *True faith is unlimited in its potential.* The descriptions of faith in verses 33 to 35 presume the presence of vision. **"Where there is no vision, the people perish" (Proverbs 29:18)**. Faith refuses to accept the "inevitable"; it marches to a different beat of the drum than what the masses hear. Who would have thought that faith could change the destiny of a nation? But faith has **"subdued kingdoms"** again and again (v. 33). True faith not only transforms lives, but changes nations. Martin Luther's vision of justification by "faith alone" transformed the *soul*. John Calvin took things a step further; he saw that the same doctrine could change *nations*. According to Harry Emerson Fosdick, to read Western civilization apart from Calvin is to read history with "one eye shut."

So unlimited is faith in what it can do, says our writer, that it reverses the course of nature. **"Women received their dead raised to life again" (v. 35)**. This is faith mocking the "inevitable." To grasp the nature of true faith is to *understand its opposition to nature* and the way we naturally think. Nature posits: "It cannot be done." Faith posits: "It *can*." Faith builds its domain with the stone which the **"builders refused" (Matthew 21:42)**. Faith is not threatened by the solitude of seeing what others are blind to. Faith is not intimidated by the trends slavishly followed by the unthinking majority. Nature takes its cue from what can be done; faith takes its cue from what cannot.

3. *True faith is unrewarded obedience.* Faith is not motivated to do what it does because it anticipates a certain payment in this life in return; it just *does* it. The three Hebrew young men recognized the very real possibility that God might be pleased to let the flames reduce their bodies to ashes. What lay behind their quenching **"the violence of fire" (v. 34)** was not their projection that God would reward them if they did what they did. Quite the opposite. **"If it be so, our God whom we serve is able to deliver us from the burning fiery furnace...*but if not*, be it known unto thee, oh king, that we will not serve thy gods, nor worship the golden image which thou hast set up" (Daniel 3:17-18)**.

Their faith was motivated by pure obedience, not done for the purpose of seeking a reward. It did not enter their minds that their obedience was anything spectacular. As our Lord put it, **"So likewise ye, when ye shall have done all those things which are commanded you, say, We are unprofitable servants: we have done that which was our duty to do"** **(Luke 17:10).**

Obedience, then, is its own reward. Faith knows this. Faith is obedient to the God who gave it. This obedience is not contingent upon results or calculated success. It is not at work because it "works"; it is at work because its motivation is pleasing God.

What faith *does,* then, is in a sense accidental—that is, its purpose is not to achieve a certain result. Rather, faith merely "happens" to achieve the result. Faith is unrewarded obedience. What God may do on top of faith's obedience—whether enabling one to **"escape the edge of the sword"** or **"stop the mouths of lions"**—is not our prerogative but His. **"Though He slay me, yet will I trust Him" (Job 13:15).** Thus, **"others were tortured, not accepting deliverance; that they might obtain a better resurrection" (v. 35).** Faith obeys God. God determines the results. Faith wouldn't have it any other way.

Faith Facing Persecution

Our writer brings his glorious chapter to a close by letting surface what has been implicit all along: *Faith is always facing the possibility of persecution.*

All the men and women described in Hebrews 11 were constantly walking on the edge of persecution. If anyone has the impression that faith *always* escapes the edge of the sword or *always* turns **"to flight the armies of the aliens" (v. 34),** he has a distorted picture of the nature of faith. For accepting torture requires as much faith as stopping the mouths of lions. Our writer therefore brings this chapter on faith to an end by making this prospect not fearful, but very dear indeed. There is a faith that *escapes* the edge of the sword; yet there is an equally valiant faith that *submits* to the edge of the sword.

I offer three principles on the matter of persecution:

1. *Avoid persecution if you can, but welcome it if it must come.* Not one of the figures of Hebrews 11 had a "persecution complex." There is no place for would-be martyrs in the kingdom of God. One of the mistakes of the church has been to glorify its martyrs, however, these men and women were no different from us. They did what they had to do—so would we. Greatness is not achieved by creating the time and circumstances that afford greatness, but by faithfully following the principles of faith.

Persecution, then, must never be sought—though if you look for it, you will probably find it. Go out of your way to avoid it, whether it be verbal or nonverbal persecution. Why do you suppose our writer has saved this subject of persecution for the end? Because it should always be the last resort. If persecution *must* come, welcome it, for this is a sign you are a child of God. **"All that will live godly in Christ Jesus shall suffer persecution" (II Timothy 3:12)**. If Providence—time and circumstances—elevates you to the high honor of suffering for Christ, accept such persecution with dignity. **"Happy are ye; for the spirit of glory and of God resteth upon you" (I Peter 4:14)**.

2. *Grace will always be equal to the test.* **"As thy days, so shall thy strength be" (Deuteronomy 33:25)**. People used to speak of what they called "dying grace." If you ask me what that is, my answer is: "I don't know. I've never needed it." But many who did gave the impression that it was very adequate indeed. You need special grace for special trials. We sometimes covet the marvelous experience of grace we had yesterday, but tend to forget the trial that necessitated it. If you are praying for more grace at the moment but are not getting it, perhaps you have enough already.

God always supplies grace equal to the trial, but He does not necessarily cut us off from the painful reality of things. These people were **"stoned,"** and were **"tempted"**—they were **"afflicted"** and **"tormented."** Of course they felt pain. Of course they were scared. These temptations were real. When Nicholas Ridley was tied to the stake in Oxford in 1555, he was scared. It was Latimer who called to him, "Fear not, Master Ridley, and play the man; we shall this day light such a candle in England which I trust by God's grace shall never be put out." Despite the magnitude of the trial, *enough* grace was given.

3. *It is not you but God that is hated.* Knowing this will enable you to avoid developing a "persecution complex." The saints of God do not take persecution personally because they know the real reason they are being persecuted: Men hate Christ. **"If the world hate you, ye know that it hated me before it hated you" (John 15:18). "The world cannot hate you; but me it hateth, because I testify of it, that the works thereof are evil" (John 7:7).**

Persecution is nothing but a repeat performance of the cosmic battle between wickedness and righteousness. Persecution is nothing new; it is the predictable effect of man's hatred of God. Faith bears out a principle which all men hate; indeed, the believer manifests a righteousness which all men hate. It is a righteousness that is "given"; it is imputed and then imparted. This should keep every believer from being self-righteous.

If the world does not detect the *givenness* of the righteousness in you, do not worry; you will not be persecuted. If they only see "you," they will not be greatly offended—only relieved. The world is not angry with our morality; it is angry with the righteousness that comes from beyond human nature. For the righteousness that defies a natural explanation keeps them guessing and makes them afraid.

Those who create that kind of reaction in others are said to be ones **"of whom the world was not worthy."** The world does not think this, of course. The world persecutes because it thinks this is what people of faith deserve. But the root of their consternation with us is a righteousness for which there is no natural explanation. Therefore, do not forget that it was not persecution but *faith* that accounts for our writer's phrase—**"of whom the world was not worthy."** For faith has its origin from beyond nature.

There are those of whom the world *is* worthy. Who are they? They are those who think that this world is all there is. And this world is all they will get. But not so with those the writer of Hebrews has sought to describe. And not so with us if we follow the same principles that guided them.

One word can capsulate what motivated those **"of whom the world was not worthy."** It is what drove them forward despite all odds. It demonstrates that God is not ashamed to be called their God. What is this one word? He has **"prepared for them a *city*" (v. 16)**—a city. What enabled them to accomplish extraordinary things along the way was the sight, however afar off, of that city.

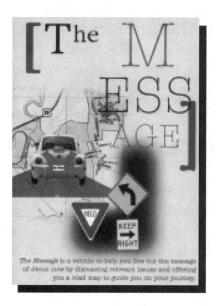

The Message™

The MorningStar Youth Journal

The Message™—for the new generation!

With contributions from both youth and adults, *The Message™* is a quarterly publication devoted to helping young people live out the message of Jesus now. In each issue, we seek to offer youth a road map to guide them on their journeys through these important days by discussing relevant issues from a biblical perspective.

US Subscriptions	**YMAG**	**$10.00**
Foreign Subscriptions	**FYMAG**	**$15.00**USD

MorningStar
SCHOOL OF MINISTRY

This is not a Bible School, but a School of Ministry devoted to the practical equipping needed for ministry in the advancing, prophetic church of the 21st century.

- MSM is a one to three year course, depending on your needs and experience.
- MSM begins with an intense one week boot camp to help prepare you for the ministry training you will receive.
- At MSM, you will be given training and practical experience working on prophetic and evangelistic teams with opportunities to participate on worship and intercessory teams.
- Courses include teaching and training in worship, children's ministry, youth ministry and missions.
- 2nd and 3rd year students teach MSM classes and MorningStar services, participate in ministry trips and outreaches and lead pastoral, prophetic or evangelistic teams.

Correspondence Course

MorningStar Ministries is aggressively accepting the challenge to equip the saints to do the work of the ministry. Understanding that not everyone who desires to be equipped can come to our Charlotte location, we are making correspondence courses available. The actual audio or video tapes of our School of Ministry classes can be experienced in your own home or church. The courses are designed so that you may work at your own pace according to your schedule.

You May Request An Application From Our MSM Office by calling (704) 542-9880, ext. 51, or by writing to MSM, 16000 Lancaster Hwy., Charlotte, NC 28277